Down with stereotypes!

Eliminating sexism from
children's literature
and school textbooks

Down with stereotypes!

Eliminating sexism from children's literature and school textbooks

Andrée Michel

Unesco

Published in 1986 by the United Nations Educational,
Scientific and Cultural Organization,
7 place de Fontenoy, 75700 Paris
Printed by Imprimerie des Presses Universitaires de France,
Vendôme

ISBN 92-3-102380-2
French edition: 92-3-202380-6
Russian edition: 92-3-402380-3

© Unesco 1986
Printed in France

Brief biography of the author

Andrée Michel holds a *doctorat d'État* in sociology (University of Paris, 1959), and is at present Director of Research at the Centre National de la Recherche Scientifique—CNRS (National Scientific Research Centre), Paris, France, where she heads the study group on Sex Roles, the Family and Human Development. She has written a number of articles published in national and international journals and has either written or supervised the writing of several books, including: *La condition de la Française d'aujourd'hui*,[1] *Activité professionnelle de la femme et vie conjugale*,[2] *Travail féminin: un point de vue*,[3] *Femmes, sexisme et sociétés*,[4] *Les femmes dans la société marchande*,[5] *Le féminisme*[6] and *Femmes et multinationales*.[7]

She is a member of several scientific societies in the fields of sociology and demography, and has taken part in many national and international symposia and meetings on the subject of equality of opportunity for girls and women in all areas, and in particular in education, training and employment.

1. Geneva, Gonthier, 1964. (Femme, 2.)
2. Paris, Centre National de la Recherche Scientifique, 1974.
3. Paris, Documentation Française, 1975. (Travaux et recherches de prospective, 54.)
4. Paris, Presses Universitaires de France, 1977. (Sociologie d'aujourd'hui.)
5. Paris, Presses Universitaires de France, 1978. (Sociologie d'aujourd'hui.)
6. Paris, Presses Universitaires de France, 1979. (Que sais-je?)
7. Paris, Karthala/Agence de Coopération Culturelle et Technique, 1981.

Preface

Much progress has been made towards recognizing the equality of women and men as a right, and a right that must be guaranteed in practice. Virtually no one today would question the desirability of this development, and decision-makers in many countries are engaged in translating it into action.

Unesco, together with several other organizations in the United Nations system, has played an important part in this development by making a point of censuring the harmful influence exerted by sexist prejudice, in society and at school, on the equality of women and men and on mutual respect between them.

This realization has been reaffirmed on many occasions, especially at the World Conference of the United Nations Decade for Women, which stated that education and training should 'contribute to a change in attitudes by abolishing traditional stereotypes of men's and women's roles and stimulating the creation of new and more positive images of women's participation in the family, the labour market and in social and public life,'[1] and urged governments 'to take all necessary measures to eliminate stereotypes on the basis of sex from educational materials at all levels'.[2]

With the twin aims of supporting efforts to counter sexist prejudice and encouraging new initiatives, Unesco launched an extensive programme to alert public opinion to the problem of sexism in children's literature and school textbooks and to encourage, promote and support action to that end. This is the background against which the present work by Andrée Michel, Director of Research at the Centre National de la Recherche Scientifique (CNRS) in Paris, is being published. Although based on personal research, it also has an international dimension inasmuch as Ms Michel backs up her conclusions by reference to studies carried out, at Unesco's request, in various regions of the world.

These national studies, listed in the References section on page 99, were conducted in seven countries (China, France, Kuwait, Norway, Peru, the Ukrainian Soviet Socialist Republic and Zambia) on the images of women and of men projected by school textbooks and children's literature. The aim was to enable the authorities in the countries concerned to obtain a clearer picture of the problem and to take appropriate action. The studies are supplemented by three regional guides, prepared for the Arab States, for Asia and the Pacific, and for North America and Western Europe, by specialists from those regions.

This publication, which Unesco hopes will be used as a practical aid to tracking down and eliminating sexist prejudice in school textbooks, is intended particularly for planners, writers, illustrators and publishers of textbooks and children's books in general, since it is they who have the power to influence attitudes and hence to develop a sense of equality and respect for all. It should also be of interest to readers of both sexes throughout the world who feel concerned by this issue.

1. *Report of the World Conference of the United Nations Decade for Women: Equality, Development and Peace, Copenhagen, 14–30 July 1980*, p. 34, New York, United Nations, 1980. (A/CONF.94/35.)
2. Ibid., p. 109.

Andrée Michel, whom Unesco wishes to thank, is responsible for the choice and presentation of the facts contained in this book and for the opinions expressed therein, which are not necessarily those of Unesco, and do not commit the Organization. She is also responsible for the new terminology adopted.

Contents

Introduction 11

Part one: Sexist stereotypes in society and at school

1. Sexist stereotypes in society and in children's literature 15
Definition 15
The purpose of sexist stereotypes 17
Propagation and credibility of sexist stereotypes 18
Literature for children and teenagers 20
The effects of sexist stereotypes 23

2. Sexist stereotypes at school and in school textbooks 25
The various forms of sexism at school 25
The effects of sexism on schoolchildren 31

Part two: Eliminating sexism from children's literature and school textbooks

Introduction 47

3. Identifying sexism in school textbooks and children's literature 48
Analytical checklist for the identification of sexism 49
Outline for a simplified sexist stereotypes checklist 54
Outline for a simplified sexist occupational activities checklist 57
Latent sexism in social references and in the activities of male and female characters 57

4. Producing non-sexist children's literature and school textbooks	59
Brief guidelines for the production of non-sexist publications	59
5. Action to eliminate sexism in the school system	64
Action towards ministries or departments of education and culture	64
Action towards administrative and non-teaching personnel in schools	65
Action towards teaching staff and educators	66
Action towards guidance counsellors and education advisers	70
Action towards pupils	72
6. Action to eliminate sexism outside the school system	75
Action towards publishers, authors and illustrators of school textbooks and children's literature	75
Action towards local authorities and parents	79
Action towards the media, the general public and associations	80
Action towards employers	81
Assessment of the impact of action against sexism in children's literature and school textbooks	82
Conclusion	85
Appendixes	
1. Unesco series of national studies on portrayal of men and women in school textbooks and children's literature: tentative suggestions for research	87
2. Guidelines for equal treatment of the sexes in McGraw-Hill Book Company publications	92
3. Recommendations to textbook authors and illustrators, drawn up by Fernand Nathan, publishers, June 1980	98
References	99
Select bibliography	103

Introduction

Sexism—or practices, prejudices and ideologies that treat one sex as inferior to the other in worth and status—is still one of the most serious ills afflicting humanity, because besides making one sex (usually women) suffer, it deprives all societies of a vast intellectual and human potential that has hitherto been ignored or despised. The feminist movements brought the concept of 'sexism' into use to denote discriminatory practices and ideologies directed against women, and they strove to make people realize that such phenomena are no less unjust and reprehensible than those directed against individuals on grounds of race, religion or political affiliation. In creating the concept of 'sexism' to stigmatize discrimination against one of the sexes, when such discrimination had previously been viewed as the consequence of a natural order in which different functions and roles were assigned to women, society took a considerable step forward. By using this concept, society shows that it no longer views differences used to subordinate the female sex as being ordained by God or as deriving from a natural biological order, but now sees them as the result of unjust social treatment of women. Society further recognizes the need for a new, just status for women, equal in dignity to that of men in all areas of life: family, work, social relations, politics, art, access to technology, science, sport, etc.

As in the past, feminists have been the pioneers in condemning discrimination against women, especially from 1965 onwards. And since in most countries women constitute the majority of primary-school, and in some cases secondary-school, teachers and, as educators, tend more often than men to buy school textbooks and children's books and are more actively involved in children's schooling, it is not surprising that they were the first to notice the sexist prejudice and stereotypes that abound in the texts and pictures of those books. Hence their research and their determined efforts to point out this kind of sexism and deplore it, more particularly in the Scandinavian countries, the United Kingdom, France and the United States.

This line of attack on sexism was dealt with in a large number of different publications that attracted the attention of the public authorities and those involved in education: teachers, parents and publishers. But it was not desirable to confine these activities to such a small geographical area. In keeping with its worldwide mission to promote equality of opportunity for girls and women in education, Unesco commissioned a series of studies in every continent, in order to obtain an overall view of sexist prejudice in school textbooks and children's literature. These national studies provided a wealth of material which made it possible to highlight sexism in the texts and illustrations of school textbooks and children's books. The studies also contain thoroughgoing discussion on how to identify sexism and how to produce non-sexist children's books. Unesco's second initiative was to commission a book that would offer a checklist for identifying sexism in schoolbooks and books for children, and would make recommendations on how to avoid it.

Having been asked to write this book, I did not fail to take advantage of the mine of information already available in the studies prepared at Unesco's request. Indeed, I felt that the message to be brought home to the various governments and education authorities urging each country to make an effort to reduce, and ultimately to eliminate, sexism in school textbooks would probably be better received and would make a greater impact if I could offer African, Asian or Latin American readers not only research findings and guidelines originating in Western countries, but also those of socialist countries and countries in Asia, Africa and Latin America. The universality of sexism, i.e. women's subordinate status, maintained primarily by sexist prejudice and stereotypes, calls for a universal counter-attack: hence the need to give due weight to the observations and suggestions of the Asian, Soviet, African and Latin American participants in Unesco's studies.

It would have been unthinkable to leave untapped the tremendous documentary resources contained in the national studies. Accordingly, in every chapter, the reader travels between continents and countries: from China to Peru via the Ukrainian Soviet Socialist Republic, Lebanon, Kuwait, Zambia, Norway, France, Canada and the United States. Each of these countries has thus made an indirect but useful contribution to the writing of this book.

It should be noted that, in order to comply with the recommendations for preparing non-sexist school textbooks and children's books, I have taken certain liberties with the French dictionary, feminizing certain nouns that have not yet been given a feminine form in the dictionary (e. g. *auteure* as the feminine of *auteur*; *professeure/professeur*; *ingénieure/ingénieur*; *écrivaine/écrivain*, etc.). These forms are already accepted and used in some French-speaking countries. New terms are made familiar through usage, and not by attaching undue importance to obsolete rules of grammar. The issue at stake, equality between the sexes, is well worth a couple of infringements of the grammatical orthodoxy that gives one sex precedence over the other (the 'second sex'), as do most grammars in other languages. But times have changed, and there should no longer be a 'second sex', whether in the language or in the content, texts, or illustrations of school textbooks and children's literature.

The reader may be surprised to find no breakdown of the generic concept of 'children's books' into different categories of publication for the purpose of analysing sexist stereotypes (picture books for small children, illustrated story-books, adventure books, historical fiction, science fiction, strip cartoons, magazines, etc.). Nor is there any breakdown of school textbooks according to subject, this being an impossible task in the space permitted. Moreover, the Unesco-commissioned and other studies only rarely made such a distinction, and, when they did, the same sexist trend was discernible in all cases. Both the tests for identifying sexism and the guidelines for writing non-sexist texts can be validly extended to cover all school textbooks and all literature for children and teenagers.

This book does not claim to be exhaustive or to provide magic formulae for the promotion of equality between men and women; the universality of the problem of sex stereotypes should not blind us to its difficulty, or to the diversity of approaches that it is possible to adopt, depending on the sociocultural context. It is therefore a matter for the public authorities, teachers and indeed all interested parties in every country to choose the measures they consider most appropriate in order to eliminate the stereotyped images associated with girls and women, on the one hand, and with boys and men, on the other, in school textbooks and literature for children, and to introduce more positive and enhancing images of girls and women. These new images can, I think, be effective in helping to develop attitudes in young people and adults that are conducive to equality and mutual respect between men and women, thus furthering not only economic and social development but also the well-being of individuals in human society.

Part one

Sexist stereotypes in society and at school

1. Sexist stereotypes in society and in children's literature

Definition

Many similarities exist between the concepts of racism and sexism. While racism entails the use of discriminatory images, attitudes, behaviour and stereotypes against a certain ethnic group, sexism entails the practice of various forms of discrimination based on sex. A person can be called 'sexist' if his or her thoughts and behaviour patterns are to some degree consciously infused with sexism. Even more explicitly: 'Sexism is . . . [an] attitude which demeans, excludes, under-represents and stereotypes people on the basis of gender' [1, p. 15].[1] In an even broader sense, 'sexism is a course of action which favours one sex over another. Sex-related stereotypes are, for example, favourable to men' [2, p. 3].

Prejudice, which may be defined as a belief, or an *a priori* opinion, imposed by the environment, the times and education, closely resembles the definition of stereotype, which is 'something repeated or reproduced without variation—something corresponding to a fixed or general pattern and lacking individual distinguishing features or qualities; a standardized mental picture held in common by members of a group, and representing an overly simplified opinion, affective attitude or uncritical judgement' [3, p. 6]. Racist and sexist stereotypes alike can be conveyed through a judgement, a feeling or an image: racist stereotypes referring to an ethnic group, sexist stereotypes referring to gender. According to Shestakov: 'the stereotype ignores the reality of individual differences and produces normative, standard values, and very often reflects common prejudices' [3, p. 6].

In so far as the stereotype reflects an unduly general and over-simplified viewpoint, it is rightly described as a negative phenomenon that distorts reality. It is unfounded in that, lacking any scientific proof whatsoever, it ascribes certain characteristics to an ethnic group or sex on the grounds of an ostensibly 'natural' distinction. Biological differences do, of course, exist between ethnic groups (e.g. skin colour) and between the sexes, but such differences do not warrant such summary judgements as attributing superior intelligence to certain ethnic groups over others, or to one sex over the other.

If we take Dunnigan's definition of a stereotype [2, p. 3]: 'a rigid impersonal model on the basis of which images or behaviour are automatically reproduced', it is easy to see how the same concept can be used not only as a noun and an adjective, to qualify an image, attitude or type of behaviour, but also as a verb, signifying the very act of creating a stereotype.

Sexist stereotypes of males and females tend to deny the worth of women and girls and to over-emphasize the importance of men and boys. Moreover, a certain uniformity in the presentation of female or male characters is noticeable, creating a sort of barrier between the two groups which results in the characteristics peculiar to one being criticized by the other. In other words, male and female characters are stereotyped to such an extent that the glorification of men inevitably implies the degradation of women.

Sexist stereotyping of the behaviour of men and

---

1. Numbers in square brackets refer to the References section on pages 99–101.

women, favouring men to the detriment of women, is to be found in virtually all societies today. A striking example is furnished by the writer Jan Morris who, after a sex-change operation, noticed a dramatic change in her own attitudes:

We are told that the social gap between the sexes is narrowing, but I can only report that having, in the second half of the twentieth century, experienced life in both roles, there seems to me no aspect of existence, no moment of the day, no contact, no arrangement, no response, which is not different for men and for women. . . . [Everything] constantly emphasized my change of status. . . . The more I was treated as a woman, the more woman I became. I adapted willy-nilly. If I was assumed to be incompetent at reversing cars, or opening bottles, oddly incompetent I found myself becoming [4, pp. 148–9].

In other words, all stereotypes, even those that seem innocuous, exert a considerable influence on those whom they label.

Content of stereotypes

We have seen that stereotypes may take the form of images, attitudes, feelings and activities. As regards their content, stereotypes can refer to the physical characteristics of a group (e.g. women or men), its members' intellectual, emotional or volitional qualities, or certain aspects of its position in society.

The statement 'men are aggressive' is sexist, as it implies that aggression is innate to men, while ignoring the influence of early childhood education, which encourages boys to direct their aggressiveness outwards against others, while girls are encouraged to stifle this feeling, or to turn it against themselves.

Texts and illustrations which depict women solely as wives and mothers, existing only in terms of their relations with their husbands and children, are sexist in that the following facts are left out of account: not all women are wives and mothers—single women (the unmarried, widowed, divorced, separated, etc.) are persons in their own right; not all women's lives can be summed up uniquely in terms of their relations with their husbands and children—in the world as a whole, there are many more who lead independent social lives as well, either with neighbours or with colleagues at their place of employment.

The systematic depiction of the man as head of the household above his wife and children is a sexist stereotype, since in many families men and women share decision-making about their home, children and respective occupations. At the same time, the claim that men are incapable of looking after children and behaving lovingly towards them is also a sexist view, as men are equally capable of showing tenderness towards their children and taking care of them.

Sexist stereotypes operate according to a strict binary logic, assigning to women the qualities and shortcomings denied to men, while men find themselves credited with the positive and negative qualities denied to women. It goes without saying that this assignment of sexist stereotypes is biased, and that men are credited with having more positive features (courage, intelligence, self-confidence, professional competence, a taste for risk and adventure, the spirit of initiative, efficiency), while women are seen as lacking these 'manly' qualities, while possessing their own 'feminine' virtues which men supposedly lack.

Explicit and latent stereotypes

The national studies prepared at the request of Unesco distinguish between explicit (written and spoken) stereotypes and implicit, or latent, stereotypes.

In the category of explicit stereotypes, Bisaria [5] cites school curricula which discriminate between 'typically women's subjects' and 'typically men's subjects'. Such stereotypes stand in the way of equal educational opportunities for boys and girls, since children are advised to follow certain courses of study, not with reference to their aspirations or potential, but exclusively on the basis of sexist stereotypes.

Moreover, the fact that it is specified in school curricula that girls should be guided towards arts-and-crafts work, whereas boys should attend woodwork classes, is evidence of an explicit sexist stereotype, as this educational dichotomy amounts to denying both sexes a free choice of practical work.

It would, of course, be inappropriate to channel all boys into handicrafts and all girls into woodwork, but it is important to give pupils the freedom to choose their elective subjects as they see fit. Openly expressed sexist stereotypes exist not only in institutions but in daily customs which discriminate between boys and girls. For example, although there is no law to that effect, parents are frequently heard telling their sons: 'Big boys don't cry'. Such stereotyped judgements are designed to train the boy to repress his feelings, whereas the expression of the same emotion by a girl is not discouraged.

Latent sexism occurs not so much in speech or writing as in social attitudes and behaviour that differ according to the sex of the individual. So a girl can be complimented on her pretty dress, while praise for doing well at school is reserved for boys. In this example, attitudes towards children are not combined with discriminatory judgements favouring one sex over the other; rather, it is the attitudes themselves that are discriminatory. The assumption is that girls should be trained to please others, while boys should be prepared for social success.

Latent sexism is also conveyed by omission; that is, when the portrayal of one sex is confined to specific qualities and roles. This type of sexism is given special emphasis in the guide prepared by Abu Nasr et al.: 'Hidden [sexist] messages ... may be conveyed in disguise.... Motherhood is honoured and respected, but is the only option for girls' [1, p. 16].

This last example seems to be the most prevalent illustration of implicit sexism in the media, textbooks and children's literature: women and girls are represented and valued only in their emotional, maternal and domestic roles, which by implication means that all other social roles (professional and political) are closed to them.

We find the same idea expressed in a study conducted in Quebec: 'In some cases girls are openly encouraged to believe that the goals of their adult lives will be marriage and motherhood, while boys have a much wider variety of role models, and their role as husbands and fathers is treated as an irrelevant detail' [2].

Hidden discrimination consists of providing girls with only one role model (homemaker), while a much wider range is open to boys. Informal latent sexism can also be observed in the different attitudes that parents in low-income countries adopt towards their sons and daughters. For example, book illustrations depict a small girl carrying her younger brother on her back, while an older brother plays marbles or flies a kite. The girl is obviously already conditioned to help her parents when she leaves school, while greater freedom of choice is given to boys. Parents' attitudes, whether or not accompanied by sex-stereotyped comments, make it obvious to boys that they are the superior sex, and to girls that they are somehow inferior.

The purpose of sexist stereotypes

Sexist stereotypes, like racial stereotypes, have a social function that has been studied by sociologists. It has been demonstrated that racial prejudices are the outcome of a situation of oppression and exploitation, with its roots in history. For example, when blacks were taken as slaves following the white colonial conquest, prejudices and racial stereotypes had to be invented in order to justify the oppression and domination exercised by white slaveholders. This historical precedent and the persistence of the pattern of discrimination thus established account for the fact that prejudice and racial stereotypes conveying the idea that blacks are inferior to whites have survived to this day. In short, sociologists have discovered that racial prejudices and stereotypes are the result of discriminatory practices directed against a certain ethnic group, and that such stereotypes are used as an excuse for maintaining this group in a position of inferiority (economic, cultural, social, political, etc.) [6]. However, racial stereotypes perpetrate a vicious cycle which further contributes to discriminatory practices towards the supposedly inferior ethnic group.

Sexist stereotypes are created and reproduced on the same pattern. Thus, in the West, the birth of the concept of private property, whose most obvious manifestation is money, gave rise to a new type of family unit: the bourgeois family, in which the husband was the head and administrator of the family property, while the wife was declared legally incompetent. This bourgeois family, which appeared in French law for the first time in the fourteenth century, is the successor of the feudal family in which the married woman was not considered incompetent, and was free to manage her own property, appear in court and participate in political life. In order to justify the newly declared incompetence of the bourgeois wife in the eyes of the law, the legal experts of the day borrowed the stereotype of *fragilitas sexus* (the weaker sex) from Roman law; this example goes to show that the stereotype was indeed used to support a new type of family structure, whose salient features were practices and legislation of a discriminatory nature against married women.

Later, other myths degrading women were to appear in the West. By the end of the nineteenth century, the combination of discriminatory practices used by capitalist entrepreneurs against women workers, coupled with the caging of middle-class women within the family structure, produced further sexist stereotypes concerning women. They became identified as 'housewives' and, even when they went out to work, stereotypes dictated that they were suited only for 'part-time work', earning 'pin money' [7].

It is understandable that sexist stereotypes persist in contemporary societies. In all cases, they serve to legitimize, justify and exacerbate women's position of dependence, subordination and inequality in society; on an international scale, a situation which has been summed up by the United Nations as follows:

women represent more than 50 per cent of the world population and carry out 66 per cent of the total number of working hours (paid and unpaid work); at the same time, they represent only 33 per cent of the paid labour force, as men reserve most salaried work for themselves; women occupy a tiny fraction of the top political decision-making positions at national and international levels; and they receive only one-tenth of the world's income and own less than 1 per cent of the world's property [8].

Propagation and credibility of sexist stereotypes

Since women are undervalued and downgraded all over the world, we can say that the very functioning of the social system is sexist. Merely observing this system operate and perpetuate itself is an effective means of socialization calculated to make children and adults of both sexes believe that women are the inferior sex. Morever, this system leads them to sanction all sexist stereotypes that uphold the status quo, no matter how unfair or unhealthy such a situation may be.

Within this overall social system (national or international), there are also a number of social subsystems in which children and adults live their daily lives, and which propagate sexist stereotypes whose aim is to vindicate the superiority of one sex over the other. Examples of such subsystems are the family, the school, peer groups, age-groups, the work place, the labour market, political parties, unions, associations and the media. At this point, we should examine briefly the role of some of these subsystems.

The family

In developed and developing countries alike, the family is the best medium for perpetuating sexism. Indeed, research into time devoted to work (paid and unpaid) reveals that, in all countries, women carry out more domestic chores than men, while men work more often and for longer periods of time outside the home, for a salary or a wage. Men's work is valued because it brings in money, whereas the household work of the women is undervalued, for even if it enhances the well-being of the children and the husband, it brings less income, or none at all, into the home. Here, then, is a potential cause of children's absorption of sexist stereotypes. The father is seen as superior, the mother inferior; a situation exacerbated by family legislation which designates the husband as 'head of the household' and casts him in the role of breadwinner.

The child's perception of the division of labour between the two parents is vital to the formation of his or her identity as a boy or girl. Thus, the household tasks carried out by the young mother in rural areas of the developing world are significant in girls' perception of their role: they expect to take care of their younger brothers and sisters, while boys aged 6 and over look after livestock such as goats, sheep or buffaloes [5, p. 35].

Sexist stereotypes are also inherent in parents' attitudes towards their daughters and sons. In Western countries, dolls, tea-sets, miniature brooms, dustpans or sewing machines are often bought for girls, while boys are given construction sets, mechanical toys (cars, planes, trains) or electronic games which develop skills other than those needed for housekeeping.

However, the distribution of roles within the family and the division of labour between father and mother (paid work for the father and unpaid work for the mother) are not the only means of inculcating sexist stereotypes in the family.

The attitudes, behaviour and feelings that parents have towards their children differ according to the sex of the child. In many countries, the birth of a boy is a cause for great celebration, while that of a girl is greeted with silence, or may even earn the wife reproaches from her husband. This sexist stereotyping is compounded by the discrimination to be observed in parents' attitudes and behaviour towards their children, particularly in societies or social classes where material goods are scarce. In these families, boys often receive larger portions of food than do girls, and the best pieces of meat are saved for them. Moreover, girls' schooling is more readily sacrificed than that of boys, which results in higher levels of illiteracy for women than for men.

School

Sexism is also learned in school, in particular through the sexist stereotypes found in textbooks. This issue is discussed in Chapter 2.

Peer groups and age-groups

Peer groups are also 'schools for sexism'. Simply by observing their playmates' games, young children of both sexes learn that rough, noisy street games like football are reserved for boys, while girls' games are confined to the house, or must remain more discreet (playing with dolls, or hopscotch on the pavement). Peer groups encourage stereotyped activities in children of both sexes. 'Acceptance by the peer group entails conforming and subscribing to the values and goals of the group, and deviance is punished by the threat of withdrawal of support and friendship' [5]. The same study goes on to point out:

Many adolescent girls believe that the development of their intellectual abilities will have only negative results and should not be pursued, since they will always be less important and less capable than most men. Boys, on the other hand, are pressured to attain athletic success and high academic achievement [5, p. 33].

The age-group usually coincides with the peer group, and propagates sexist stereotypes in the same way.

The labour market

The labour market segregates men and women in occupations as well as on the shop floor, to such an extent that some occupational branches, professions and trades are assigned exclusively to women, and others to men. Furthermore, the same jobs performed by men and women do not earn them equal pay: women who show manual dexterity on electronic equipment assembly lines, or on sewing machines, are not rewarded by salary increases or promotion, as are men who perform jobs requiring physical strength or work with machine tools. Higher professional qualifications in blue-collar jobs (skilled or highly skilled categories) are reserved for men, while women tend to be classified as unskilled or semi-skilled workers, and remain so all their lives. In all occupations, manual or intellectual, positions of authority and responsibility are given to men, as it is assumed that women are not interested in such positions or are incapable of taking on such responsibilities.

Thus the world of work, too, is sexist. The child has only to look around to be convinced of the 'inferiority' of women.

Politics and the media

Politics and the media also convey this concept of inequality. Through the media, children observe that men occupy top positions in government, parliament, political and union assemblies, and international organizations, whereas women are nowhere to be seen, or, when they are present, are portrayed as legions of secretaries, typists or interpreters, in subordinate or invisible positions, with no voice of their own. An extensive study has been conducted under the auspices of Unesco on the media as transmitters of sexist messages to children and to the general public [9]. This study reveals that in countries utterly different from one another, all over the world, representations of men and women in the media are based on male and female sexist stereotypes.

Literature for children and teenagers

Literature written for children and teenagers is one of the most effective means of communicating standards, values and ideologies. Sexist indoctrination begins with picture books designed for pre-school children, before they can read and write. Comic strips, illustrated stories, adventure novels and children's magazines are leafed through or read, at home (when parents can afford them), at school (where they are used as instructional materials), or in recreation centres for children (youth centres, clubs, public and private recreation centres, children's and adult's libraries, etc.).[1]

Deeply concerned by the serious problem of the influence exerted by children's books and textbooks on the development of sexist attitudes and behaviour in young people, in 1981 Unesco embarked on a series of national studies on the portrayal of men and of women in textbooks and children's literature, with a view to determining the causes of that influence, arousing awareness in the minds of the general public and the national authorities, and proposing appropriate solutions.

The prevalence of sexist stereotypes has been confirmed by all the studies carried out under this project, in countries throughout the world. The study conducted in China speaks of the efforts made by authors of children's and teenagers' literature in that country to eliminate sexist stereotypes from their writing, especially since 1979 [10]. However, the Chinese Ministry of Culture admits that vestiges of sexist stereotypes still remain. Although Chinese women and girls are shown as having access to a number of occupations which, in the past, were considered to be men's by right, the Chinese woman's position in the family is not free from sexist stereotyping. Moreover, the authors of this report observe that in books set in schools, principals are more frequently men than women. Where community life is the backdrop to the story, officials and executives are more often men. In addition, a small number of children's books still exist in which 'boys and men are portrayed as the creators and decision-making people, while girls and women are usually presented as "passive" characters in a subordinate position' [10, p. 49].

All these sexist stereotypes are attributed to the remnants of the feudal mentality formerly prevalent in China. Be that as it may, the following observations are concerned with contemporary texts:

Of the 31 stories published in the 1981 *Selection of Children's Literature*, which is fairly influential in China and is a collection of outstanding works from various places, two-thirds portray the images of boys as the leading characters and one-third describe girls as the leading characters.... Ten short stories reflecting children's life and eight infants' stories were published in 1981 in *Juren*, a large journal of children's literature. Of these 18 pieces, 12 present boys as the leading characters, accounting for two-thirds of the total, while six, or one-third, portray girls.... *Children's Literature*, published by the China Children's Publishing House, carried 85 short stories in 1981 (not including foreign stories translated into Chinese) of which 30 or 35.3 per cent portray females as the leading characters [10, p. 51].

The study conducted in the Ukrainian Soviet Socialist Republic [11] reveals that, in children's literature, women are portrayed as often as men in the role of responsible and courageous individuals in social

1. This type of reading material, which is extremely influential in the development of young people's attitudes and behaviour, is not discussed in the present report; it warrants a separate in-depth study.

and occupational roles. However, this positive aspect of children's literature must be qualified, as 'stereotypes of importance'[1] still linger and are evidence of a discriminatory attitude towards women and girls. Such stereotypes convey the superiority of one sex over the other in one of the three fields studied: political and social roles, occupational and family roles, and characteristics attributed to each sex.

Thus, while the numbers of men and women portrayed in professional roles are almost equal in Ukrainian children's literature (5 per cent more men than women), it is also true that men and women do not have the same occupations. Despite the many different types of work available, it seems that women nearly always work in spheres that involve interpersonal relations or the natural world, while men are portrayed primarily in jobs requiring technical skills. Moreover, the positive heroes of children and adults alike are more often men than women [11, p. 24]. On the other hand, family roles represent a 'stereotype of importance' for women more than for men. This can be explained by conventional stereotypes from the past which assigned more extensive 'duties' in household management and child care to women than to men [11, p. 25].

The authors of the Ukrainian report observe that in poetry and prose as well as in the illustrations of children's books, women appear almost as often as men (although more often in illustrations than in written texts). Moreover, no literary works intended for children 'emphasize in any way physical, intellectual or moral superiority of one sex over the other' [11, p. 27]. On the contrary: the individual personality traits of each character, whether positive or negative, are developed fully. However, this absence of negative references to women and girls does not offset the staying power of sexist stereotypes. For example, emphasis is placed on different character traits in boys and in girls. Examples of this sexist stereotyping may be found in children's literature:

Boys often have their own games, their own interests and aspirations. For instance, they like fishing, football, they are enthusiastic about machines. Girls like to pick flowers and berries, they are fond of needlework, they help mother about the house. Boys are quicker, girls on most occasions are quiet. Girls do better in singing, dancing and poetry reciting. Boys are more successful in sports, chess, drawing, technical designing [11, p. 28].

Similarly, for adults, one can often observe

the stereotype of a man-defender of Motherland, a chivalrous man freeing the woman from exhausting physical work, creating favourable conditions for her intensive contacts with children [11, p. 31].

On the other hand, the Ukrainian study points out that in children's magazines, where women feature more often than men, sexist and non-sexist roles in society are equally distributed between women and men. According to the authors, this results in a sort of balance, despite the frequency of stereotyped images of the two sexes in children's literature and illustrations [11, pp. 31–2].

The study carried out in Norway [12] attempts to uncover 'hidden messages' as well as explicit ones, as they, too, put across certain forms of sexism. The results of this study can be summed up as follows [12, pp. 98 et seq.]:

In stereotypes the nuclear family, comprising a father, mother and children, predominates, while there are few or no families with widowed or divorced parents, single parents or orphans. These groups are thus placed beyond the pale.

The distribution of family roles is extremely conventional: while the man seems able to perform several roles at the same time (i.e. being a father and having a professional career), the woman is nearly always portrayed as being only a housewife and mother. The consequences of such a portrayal are, firstly, to increase the tendency to inflate the man's role by pretending that certain tasks can be performed by him alone, whereas in reality women do share such tasks, and, secondly, because the scene of the action is confined to the home, to undervalue the work carried out by women both inside and outside the home.

No alternative seems to be open to women. Unlike men, who are given active, responsible, heroic roles, women are described as mothers, wives or assistants—more often than not in a passive role.

---

1. 'The term "stereotype of importance" is used to designate an opinion which has become conventional in literature and life about superiority of one sex over the other in any sphere of human activity' [11, p. 19].

It would appear that for women there is no other option, for not one of the texts studied portrays a woman pursuing a non-traditional role.

These role models are highly idealized, and far removed from the reality experienced by children in their everyday lives. When exposed to these texts and illustrations, children enter a neutral and naïve world, devoid of tension, desire, passion, etc.

The frequent use of such grammatical forms as the neuter, the plural and the passive voice in descriptions of activities tends to make women's work 'invisible', especially in the home.

In conclusion, Norwegian children's literature portrays men as active and responsible, and women as wives and mothers who are passive, not to say irresponsible.

In France, sexist stereotypes have been found in children's literature for all age-groups, ranging from pre-school to adolescence. Béreaud's research [13] has revealed that even picture books for toddlers, who cannot yet talk, read or write, are filled with sexist images that indoctrinate children before they are able to develop an objective viewpoint. In two series produced by major French publishers of children's books, one can learn that Daddy earns money to support the family, while Mummy takes care of the house; that male occupations have an aura of power, prestige, authority and technical expertise, while female occupations require few qualifications and are underpaid (no mention is ever made of the occupations open to French women today, in skilled work, the professions, the arts, etc.). Four major themes emerge where men and boys are concerned: independence, success, competence and comradeship. Women, on the other hand, are most often described in negative or ambiguous terms: 'Little boys are allowed to run free and expand their knowledge, while little girls stay at home, learning to be docile and preparing for their future role as housewives' [13, p. 20]. These examples are glaring proof that sexism has been inculcated into children even before they reach nursery school.

The research done by Chombart de Lauwe has shown that the overshadowed and inferior images of girls and women in books and illustrated magazines for children in the 7-to-14 age-group in France is not the exception but the rule, and that sexism is well to the fore. Boys are portrayed twice as often as girls in roles requiring a spirit of adventure. Only 40 per cent of girls mentioned in novels and magazines perform adult tasks, as compared with 70 per cent of boys; 29 per cent of girls are shown as having submissive attitudes towards adults, as opposed to 17 per cent for boys. The higher degree of dependence that French parents expect of their daughters as opposed to their sons is thus reflected in children's books and magazines. In addition, boys are portrayed 10 per cent more often than girls as being intelligent, which is also an indication of the importance attached to boy's education compared with that of girls [14].

More recently, the French section of the World Federation of Teachers' Unions, having carried out a survey of twenty books in children's series (focusing on their portrayal of the status of men and women, character traits attributed to them and illustrations) came to the following conclusion:

It is no exaggeration to say that, in essence, children's literature [books and comics] brings to life for children the most conventional image conceivable of mums, dads, boys and girls—including those books which flaunt the trappings of modernity . . . we have to admit that the worst sexist images tended to occur in those [books] that were most mediocre by literary standards, i.e. in the writing itself and in the overall structure of the book. Sexism thus goes hand in hand with a cliché-ridden style, and indeed we found many of these books to be not so much written for children as inherently childish [15, p. 13].

Moreover, the authors of this study observe that there is a growing trend towards standardization in children's literature. This phenomenon is due in part to the proliferation of children's books and the growing number of foreign-language translations (five books out of every seven). In fact, there seems to be a tendency to erase all cultural or individual characteristics from children's literature, leaving only the 'skeleton key' of the original story:

So we should not be surprised to find that in these books the women, too, conform strictly to stereotypes which may be negative but which have, alas, features that are almost universally recognized [15, p. 13].

The effects of sexist stereotypes

Sexist stereotypes, themselves a product of the inequality between the sexes, in turn become the source of further discrimination between the sexes. The younger the child, the less well equipped he or she is to resist the powerful stereotypes that incline him or her to see the opposite sex as having conventional attributes, qualities or failings. Thus, young children are led to attribute mythical qualities to boys, and to look down on girls. The following case was reported by the mother of Sylvie (5 years old). Sylvie is stronger and more aggressive than her nursery-school friend Etienne, a boy of the same age. Sylvie even wins fights with Etienne occasionally, but this does not keep her from declaring: 'I'd like to be a boy because boys are stronger', while Etienne, adopting the same stereotype, adds: 'We're stronger because we're men . . . little girls are cute.' Thus, at the age of 5, Sylvie and Etienne have already learned to think and speak in terms of sexist stereotypes—to the point of denying that, in their relationship, Sylvie is stronger than Etienne.

A French study [16] has revealed that, by the age of 3 or 4, children of both sexes have already internalized their parents' preferences in terms of toys and clothing. Such preferences may well be called sexist, as parents buy certain categories of toys and clothes according to the sex of the child, and not according to the child's personal preferences.

Research conducted among children aged 7 to 11 and attending primary school has revealed the effects of sexist stereotypes. In the United States, boys in this age-group have a highly stereotyped idea of themselves: they value strength, rough games, competitive sports, stamina and competence (climbing trees, building fires, being better at arithmetic and spelling than girls, etc.). Generally speaking, they suffer from anxiety, since they are constantly afraid of resembling girls in any way, and they perceive girls in terms of negative stereotypes: cowardly, easily frightened, concerned with trivial things, playing with dolls, sewing, cooking and taking care of children.

The career choices of, for example, American boys and girls in the 7-to-11 age-group are as stereotyped as their view of character traits peculiar to each sex. The sexist stereotypes in picture books lead children to repudiate the real world in which they live. An example of this is the case of a 7-year-old American girl who, after looking at a series of pictures showing male doctors and female nurses, said: 'I can't be a doctor; I can only be a nurse. My book says so' [17]. These sexist images and stereotypes have the formidable power of making girls censor their own ambitions and potential, and curb their professional goals in order to fit into conventional stereotyped professions assigning women subordinate positions and low salaries (nurses, salesgirls, secretaries, typists, etc.).

In India, 'men identify themselves in terms of their occupation—like coolie, daily wage-worker, worker in a roadside tea shop or in an office. Women, on the other hand, tend to identify themselves in terms of other people, like parentage, spouse or mother, rather than in terms of an individual' [5, pp. 34–5).

In a comparative study carried out in Minneapolis (United States) and Bombay (India) [18], it is revealed that children's creativity is directly linked to the autonomy and freedom given them by their parents. Since parents grant less freedom to daughters than to sons in both cities, it was observed that girls in Minneapolis and Bombay alike showed less creativity than boys, in an exercise where they were asked to find a solution to a puzzle.

Thus, when sexist stereotypes rob girls of their independence, they inhibit their development, stand in the way of equality of opportunity and conflict with the principles of sexual equality set out in national and international charters. Moreover, society deprives itself of valuable human capital by depriving itself of the potential creativity that girls and women could develop, were they not trapped in the crippling shackles of stereotypes.

Conversely, the stereotyped images of boys that are conveyed by the media and children's literature have the effect of cutting boys and men off from their emotions and natural feelings. The cruel world in which we live is perhaps the outcome of this one-dimensional socialization of boys and men in the mould of harshness, competitiveness, aggressiveness and insensitivity [19].

Finally, it can safely be said that the research carried out in the various countries mentioned above points to the same conclusion: sexist stereotypes have a negative influence on boys as well as girls, although the latter are more seriously affected since they are portrayed as being the inferior sex. Indeed, these stereotypes prevent girls and women from developing their full intellectual, emotional and volitional potential by refusing to recognize them as human beings in their own right, equal in dignity to boys and men; they deny them a harmonious relationship with men, and prohibit them from making a full contribution to the development of the society in which they live.

2. Sexist stereotypes at school and in school textbooks

The various forms of sexism at school

The school is by no means an institution cut off from society; rather, it forms an integral part of it, having the power to instil in children the social values and norms of the period and the society in which they live. Consequently, even when governments have subscribed to the principle of sexual equality, schools continue to convey sexist stereotypes and practise discrimination against women. This contradiction appears particularly striking when we examine the images of men and women in textbooks. For example, despite the humanist ideals of equality upheld by the Zambian government, Tembo [20] points out that Zambian textbooks nevertheless contain: 'stereotypes, false images, content slurs and so on'. He feels that 'Part of the picture drawn in these books is seen by us to be more or less a correct reflection of the values and attitudes the society holds towards boys and girls' [20, p. 23]. Parents, for example, continue to give their sons' education priority over that of their daughters.

Furthermore, as the Peruvian report [21] points out, improving school curricula is only a partial solution to the problem. Thus, in all societies, discrepancies are found between the ideals set out in national constitutions and the everyday practice of discrimination within the education system.

Sexism in the structure of the education system

Children learn sexism not only from literature and school textbooks, but also from the school hierarchy. They have only to look around them to see how professional roles are unequally distributed between men and women in their own school. As observed by the Commission of European Communities [22], children in primary schools see that, while most teachers are women, administrative posts such as those of head teacher and deputy head are generally held by men. This pattern is extremely prevalent, and should not be dismissed lightly, as it teaches boys that when they grow up they will occupy high posts in education, government, the world of work and society, and that women tend to defer to men in the decision-making process. At the same time, it places a subliminal 'ceiling' on girls' ambitions.

Statistics quoted by the Commission of European Communities show that in 1976, in France, 67.7 per cent of primary-school teachers were women, while only 41 per cent of primary-school principals were women. For Italy, these figures were 68 and 31 per cent respectively; in the United Kingdom 76.5 and 42.9 per cent, and in Ireland 71.8 and 52 per cent (heads and deputy heads included). This sexist hierarchy is reproduced in the secondary-school system, particularly as, in the interests of co-education, boys' and girls' schools have been integrated, so that there is now an even smaller proportion of women in secondary-school headships. In addition, the majority of school inspectors are men. This is bound to build up the stereotype of the man in control, as seemingly women are capable of occupying only subordinate positions, both in the education system and in society.

Bisaria [5] points out that sexist stereotypes in Indian formal education should be weeded out from the structure and the implementation of the curriculum: in other words, from the planning stage to the classroom. Moreover, close scrutiny of Indian culture soon reveals obstacles which either keep girls from attending school in the first place or induce them, sooner or later, to drop out; for example, the distance between home and school, whether the teacher is a man or a woman, the timetable, the curriculum, or an early marriage.

In India, sexist stereotypes concern first and foremost the curriculum, which

> implies all that happens in the educational system at the formal level, from early childhood education to university and higher education. Curriculum includes classroom programme(s) as much as out-of-class activities from playgrounds to assemblies; from project work to university and college extension programmes; from youth training programmes to social service camps [5, pp. 38–9].

The author of this survey therefore suggests examining the sexist stereotypes which occur in all the different fields connected with the education system, without exception. She quotes as an example the vocational education available to girls and to boys, which is determined on the basis of a stereotyped view of their future roles at work and in society (sewing and cooking for girls, wood and metalworking for boys, etc.).

Sexism in the teacher/pupil relationship

For many years, research conducted in the United States and the United Kingdom has revealed that there is a difference in teachers' behaviour towards boys and towards girls.

The Peruvian study [21], carried out by the Peruvian National Commission for Unesco, is based on a teacher survey conducted in four schools located in different parts of the city of Lima. The aim of the study was to observe the various possible factors (socio-economic background, urban-coastal or Andean regions) which might influence teachers' behaviour towards their pupils, to examine children's reading habits and to study their concepts of male and female roles. The fifty-two teachers interviewed were selected from thirteen classes in the four schools and were divided according to whether their pupils were in first grade (6-year-olds), third grade (8-year-olds) or fifth grade (10-year-olds).

While aware that the sexist stereotypes in textbooks did not in fact reflect real-life situations, the teachers felt that the problem was not serious, as they considered it to be the responsibility of the teacher to explain to his or her pupils that girls are just as capable as boys [21, p. 79]. I believe that this attitude underestimates the importance of textbooks, while at the same time overrating the role of the teacher in the battle against sexism. Moreover, it is clear that these teachers have an ambiguous attitude towards the conventional distribution of male and female roles. While almost all of them condemn the 'macho' image (men's arrogantly high opinion of themselves compared with women), many fear that challenging traditional sex roles will mean upsetting moral values, which for them are bound up with a traditional view of the family and of the woman as the 'centre of the household'.

When the authors of the Peruvian study observed the behaviour of teachers in relation to girl pupils, they found that, in the first grade, teachers were more attentive to boys and more strict with girls, although the girls were no more disruptive than the boys. On the other hand, in the third and fifth grades (8- to 10-year-olds), teachers were more inclined to reprimand 'unruly' boys. Girls of this age were well behaved, and obeyed the rules that had been instilled in them since early childhood either by parents or by teachers, as is readily discernible in first-grade classes [21, pp. 89–91].

In the United States, research by Spaulding [23, p. 149] reveals that teachers encourage boys to express themselves, while girls are advised to stay in the background. Moreover, creativity is encouraged to a greater degree in boys than in girls. Girls are told more often than boys that they are ignorant or incapable (40 per cent of girls as opposed to 26 per cent of boys), which naturally tends to foster a general feeling of inferiority in girls [23, p. 150].

The study prepared by the French section of the World Federation of Teachers' Unions also notes the persistence of sexist stereotypes in the relations between girl students and career guidance counsellors:

Sexist ideology is strongly instrumental in the guidance and education of girls. Thus girls are considered psychologically well adapted or poorly adapted, depending on whether or not they conform to female occupational stereotypes which, in any case, all come down to low-paid jobs (even if, in some cases, a high level of education is required), in which the wage-ceiling is rapidly attained, and which carry low status: careers which, as a rule, constitute a veritable 'ghetto of underprivileged jobs' [15, p. 8].

Sexism in pupil interaction and games

Recently, a young French teacher reported that in certain suburbs of Paris, where children belong to low-income families in which the image of women remains extremely conventional, boys exhibit an extremely sexist attitude towards their female classmates. For example, one day, the boys asked their teacher to show them how to play football. The teacher agreed, on condition that the girls be allowed to play as well. The boys refused, claiming that it was not proper that girls play football. The teacher therefore refused to teach them to play. Another French example is given by Mollo [24], of the Centre National de la Recherche Scientifique (CNRS), who observes that boys will monopolize the school playground for ball games, which are theoretically forbidden when space is limited. In these cases, girls are relegated to the role of spectators. Sexist ideas about girls' position in the playground are deeply ingrained in boys' minds. In another example the boys take over electronic games, at school ousting the girls from computer terminals, which they then proceed to monopolize. So it is clear that, from a very early age, children consciously or subconsciously assimilate stereotypes concerning the appropriate place for boys and girls in the playground and the types of games that are suitable for each sex.

The Peruvian study on schoolchildren of both sexes also observes that children have already internalized sexism by the time they start primary school. For these children, men are identified with 'work', while women are identified with unpaid, lowly and monotonous chores. The image of the girl helping her mother around the house has its counterpart in the boy's desire to emulate his father. Most boys take it for granted that the husband has a job, is head of the family and has a dependent wife, even if the mother works outside the home [21, pp. 163–5].

Sexism in school texbooks: sex stereotypes

The sexism propagated at school becomes even more apparent when we examine the roles of women and men in the texts and illustrations used in school textbooks. All the sexist stereotypes that have been observed in children's literature can also be found in textbooks.

Despite Norway's long-established tradition of textbook monitoring, a detailed examination of twenty textbooks intended for pupils in their fourth and seventh years pointed to the conclusion that male and female stereotypes persist in virtually all of these textbooks [12]. Discriminatory attitudes towards girls and women are manifested in the following ways: compared with boys and men, women are mentioned less frequently in texts and appear less frequently in illustrations, and the roles assigned to them are more restricted and less varied. Their choice of role models is also more limited, and the examples and subject matter selected all indicate a prejudice in favour of boys [12, p. 88].

Discrimination against girls in Norwegian textbooks is particularly noticeable in science textbook illustrations (in Norway, science subjects are physics, chemistry and biology):

There are far more pictures of boys/men than of girls/women in the textbooks for physics, chemistry and biology for both the lower and upper secondary schools (71 per cent of all illustrations in textbooks for 13-year-olds). . . . In all the books men/boys are more active throughout; they are most often depicted in places of work, and when people are to be portrayed men/boys are used. In one of the books a man is chosen as a recurrent figure. Pictures of girls/women are used when electric hairdryers and bathroom scales are to be shown. . . . There is also a clear tendency to show only men in by far the majority of sports, not only in weight-lifting but also in such disciplines as running and long-jumping [12, p. 63].

The French study mentioned above, on sexist stereotypes in textbooks used in primary school, secondary school and technical high school (*lycée d'enseignement professionnel*), concentrates on readers and science textbooks for 8- to 13-year-olds. The authors of this study confirmed their initial hypothesis, namely, that 'at best, textbooks reflect the prevailing ideology in France today and illustrate the general atmosphere of sexism' [15, p. 20]. This observation is applicable to all the textbooks examined, in all subjects, and at all levels of schooling.

Analysis of the images and topics contained in primary-school textbooks reveals that children have no hope of escaping these sexist stereotypes. In the presentation of male and female models in textbooks:

The boys ... already have limitless possibilities for their future career. But the girls can only prepare to become 'Mummies'. So here they are, boys and girls, already labelled, straitjacketed, obliged to conform to the image imposed on them; what is expected of them is already instilled in their minds. They are ready to accept, if not all types of prejudice and discrimination, then at least the inequality of the sexes, as a matter of course.... [15, p. 19].

Science textbooks display sexism not only by featuring boys more often in illustrations and texts, but also in their very marked encouragement to boys to take science subjects, and their exclusion of girls from these. It is hardly surprising, then, to find that fewer girls than boys choose careers in science.

In physics textbooks, for example, there are many more references to a boy's world (electric trains, games, bicycles) or a man's world (factories, industry, astronomy, etc.), than to that of women. Women are seldom, if ever, mentioned, and are often shown as having no career, whereas men are portrayed as free to choose any occupation (meteorologist, roofer, mason, tile layer, runner, surveyor, etc.). The conspicuous absence of girls from such books can only suggest that the field of physics is not their territory, that girls are incompetent (apparently they cannot perform experiments correctly), that they can only be the assistants (of boys) or be semi-active (listening to boys!). All of this is part of the most sexist of stereotypes: 'women as passive beings, ready to help, dependent...' [15, p. 22].

In the natural sciences, and particularly in biology, textbook content shows a marked mechanistic dehumanization which goes hand in hand with a sexist image of men and women according to which men are strong and muscular, while women are, first and foremost, mothers [15, p. 23].

In mathematics textbooks, human characters gradually disappear as the course becomes more advanced, but, here again, boys and men are over-represented in relation to women and girls, as if to indicate to children of both sexes that mathematics is essentially a man's subject [15, p. 26].

In textbooks used in the *collèges d'enseignement secondaire* (middle schools), sexism is in evidence everywhere. In the first place, sexism is inherent in the French language, the word for 'man' being used to designate human beings as a whole. Men have jobs, while women are mothers and housewives waiting at home for their husbands and children [15, p. 28].

Literary anthologies grant little space to women writers, and give no explanation for this: 'In the extracts chosen, work, sport, friend and heroism belong exclusively to a male world' [15, p. 29].

In history textbooks, half of the human race seems to have disappeared. In geography, men's work is described, while here again, women are first and foremost wives, mothers and housewives [15, p. 30].

In middle-school science textbooks: 'examples, problems and illustrations are all sexist' [15, p. 30]. Boys solve all problems and are good at do-it-yourself work, while girls are incompetent. Men are active, women passive.

In textbooks used in secondary schools (*lycées d'enseignement général*) and in technical high schools (*lycées d'enseignement professionnel*), sexism is also apparent, despite the fact that these books vary more widely.

The authors of this French study conclude:

the most antiquated and ridiculous sexist stereotypes pursue schoolchildren and students throughout their educational career, from the first primer to the *baccalauréat*, surrounding them with an atmosphere in which men are omnipresent and have all the good roles, write history and lead the world, while women are despised, downtrodden and confined to housework and motherhood.... [As a result] the vast majority of children's story-books and school textbooks ignore all other women, i.e. those who are not passive, who bring up their children and also go out to work, who have professional responsibilities, who have a public role, who are active in tenants' associations, parents' associations, unions, political parties, etc. There is nothing or next to nothing on pioneering women, those who pilot an Airbus or break records in athletics [15, p. 44].

The Peruvian study lists the sexist illustrations and texts to be found in twenty-nine of the most widely used textbooks for the six primary classes in Lima. It observes that the over-representation of men and boys in the texts and illustrations is characteristic of all levels of primary education. In texts, for instance, 78 per cent of references to people were references to men, while only 22 per cent were to women, and in illustrations the figures were 75 and 25 per cent respectively. Moreover, the preponderance of male references increases with each successive grade in primary school, beginning with 65 per cent in first-grade textbook illustrations, and rising to 82 per cent by grade six [21, p. 18].

Personality traits specific to each sex are also strongly stereotyped: men are portrayed as brave, intelligent, patriotic and infused with a spirit of fellowship; women, on the other hand, are obedient and devoted to caring for others [21, p. 24].

In the home, women are shown as busy washing, cooking and taking care of children, while men relax or help the children with their homework. The home is depicted as the woman's special domain (out of a hundred texts in which a home is described, 70 per cent mention women, and only 30 per cent include men) [21, p. 38]. On the other hand, in illustrations of schools, 80 per cent of the characters are male, and only 20 per cent female [21, p. 40].

The world of work, as depicted in Peruvian primary-school textbooks, is peopled mainly by men: of the 104 occupations mentioned, only 8 were described as women's work, while 79 were described as men's jobs, with 17 deemed appropriate for both men and women [21, p. 43]. Professions requiring higher education are reserved almost exclusively for men. The so-called 'women's' occupations are usually an extension outside the home of women's household tasks (laundresses, dressmakers, cooks, etc.). These textbooks therefore tend to ignore reality, as no mention is made of women shopkeepers, nor of women artists, this field being depicted as reserved for men [21, pp. 44–6].

Game-playing is also shown as a male, rather than a female, activity: 31 games for boys appear in textbook illustrations, and 27 are referred to the body of the texts, while only 7 and 6 games respectively are shown for girls. Boys' activities are more varied, and require a spirit of adventure, speed and daring, and the objects used in play (bicycles, skates, balls, etc.) are exciting to play with. Girls' activities, on the other hand, seem more passive listening to the radio, visiting a friend, etc.), and they are most often shown playing with dolls or tea-sets, which are suggestive of household tasks [21, pp. 54, 63–4]. Here, once again, the world of creativity, adventure and initiative belongs to boys, not to girls.

Peruvian textbooks all but ignore the role of women in history, as 91 per cent of textual references and 89 per cent of illustrations are of men [21, p. 65].

The Zambian survey was based on an analysis of textbooks used at primary- and secondary-school levels for pupils between the ages of 7 and 15. 'The general finding was that all the books analysed are male dominant' [20, p. 4]. This domination appears both in the numerical over-representation of men to the detriment of women, in personality traits, and in the professions and functions assigned to each sex.

With respect to personality traits, the author observes that:

On the intellectual plane, men are depicted to be more intelligent, more creative, more curious, more inventive and more adventurous than women. . . . In games, women are spectators and idolizers of the agile skills of men in football and other games [20, p. 20].

The professions and occupations of male and female characters in Zambian textbooks are clearly delineated:

The men are shown to be leaders as headmasters, doctors, engineers, managers, tugging along with them women who are mere teachers, housemaids, waitresses, nurses, secretaries and housewives. The tough jobs of driver, pilot, mechanic and so on can only be done by the strong, brave and intelligent people—the men. Women are cheated, exploited and beaten by the men. Men make decisions and rule. Women follow and obey [20, p. 20].

The survey [1] of the male and female stereotypes in seventy-nine Arabic textbooks, in use in seven Arab states in 1982, dealt with Egypt, Kuwait, Lebanon, Qatar, Saudi Arabia, Tunisia and Democratic Yemen. It is interesting to note that in textbooks written in Arabic, women are depicted in the same stereotyped fashion in all countries, whether those countries be conservative, progressive, developed, developing, etc. Although Arab women are active in the most highly qualified and varied professions, they are still represented according to the traditional image of women dependent on men for economic welfare and status. Texts and illustrations in Arab textbooks describe women as confined to the house, the only careers open to them outside the house being extensions of their household duties [1, p. 12]. Their personality is also described in a stereotyped way:

Women and little girls are depicted as weak, sensitive, submissive, dependent, self-sacrificing, with no identity of their own as persons. They are presented as respected and loved martyrs who attain self-fulfilment and status through the scrupulous performance of their role expectations and functions as full-time mothers, housekeepers, dutiful wives and respectful and obedient daughters [1, p. 12].

The sexist images found in Arabic textbooks are inaccurate in that they disregard the wide variety of roles played by some women. In fact, in Arab states today, a growing number of women 'are seeking higher education, entering the labour market as administrators, artists, professionals, writers and journalists', while others are very active in voluntary organizations, and play an important role in managing their property, in agriculture, etc. [1, p. 12].

The authors of the Ukrainian study estimate that all the literary texts to be found in first-year readers portray an approximately equal number of female and male characters. Thus,

out of 127 literary works in the reader for the first class 30 titles refer to women and 36 to men. In the reader for the second class 31 titles refer to women and 34 to men. In the textbook for the 3rd class out of 150 titles 27 refer to women and 26 to men. . . . [Moreover] personality traits of male and female characters in the texts of schoolbooks are carefully delineated [11, p. 27].

In textbooks where children of both sexes exist in their own right, sexist stereotypes nevertheless occur, as boys are usually shown undertaking 'more complex and laborious tasks' than girls [11, p. 27]. In the literary passages included in textbooks, women are shown more often than men as having positive traits of character (59 per cent as opposed to 52 per cent). However, the positive features stressed for each sex are by no means the same:

men are portrayed as industrious, courageous, resolute, fearless, gallant, truthful, considerate, active, inventive, resourceful, quick, intelligent, adroit, strict, well balanced and at the same time hospitable, sympathetic, wise, affable. Traits like kindness and tenderness are very much to the fore in women. Women are affectionate, loving, trusting, solicitous, sincere, honest, outspoken, friendly, vivacious, as well as industrious, persevering, serious, strict, courageous, placid, demanding [11, p. 27].

It can therefore be claimed that in Ukrainian textbooks for first- to third-year classes, numbers of male and female characters are roughly equal, and that women are shown more often in a positive light than men. Sexist stereotypes nevertheless persist, particularly in those textbooks designed for children in the 10-to-14 age-group (fourth- to seventh-year classes): 'Stereotype of men's importance in occupations reveals itself in the comparison of these two figures—38.3 and 61.7 per cent. The first is the number of references to women's occupations or occupational aptitudes, the second—to men's' [11, p. 23].

Furthermore, the survival of the image of peasants' and craftsmen's families, where men are traditionally the breadwinners while women perform primarily domestic tasks, generates 'a psychological stereotype which brought about the situation where "women's duties" in household management, in the care of children, etc., turned out to be ever so much greater than men's' [11, p. 25].

In short, the Ukrainian study sorts the sexist stereotypes to be found in classroom materials into three categories [11, p. 34]. The first category (68 per cent) comprises stereotypes that emphasize personality traits ostensibly inherent in one sex. According to such stereotypes, men are efficient, courageous, reasonable, stubborn, etc., while in women we find a predominance of emotive traits, tenderness and solicitude.

The second category (23 per cent) includes stereotypes emphasizing family and occupational roles traditionally associated with one sex: women are housekeepers, nurses, teachers, etc.; while men are breadwinners, managers of the family budget, servicemen, lumberjacks, fitters, etc.

The third category (6 per cent) stresses the difference in the social and political activities of men and women respectively (women are passive; men are leaders).

The presence of sexist stereotypes in 55.7 per cent of Ukrainian classroom materials (textbooks and children's literature) is only slightly higher than in material which attempts to be neutral (4.5 per cent) and that which consciously tries to transcend such stereotypes (39.8 per cent) [11, p. 34].

The Kuwaiti research group [25] examined school textbooks dealing with Islam, the Arabic language, general sciences, the humanities, military education, psychology and English, as well as a number of children's books. In these textbooks, women and girls are absent altogether, or are shown very infrequently, or their image, like that of men, is strongly stereotyped. The analysis of an Arabic textbook for 6- to 7-year-olds shows that, out of fifty-six illustrations, 76 per cent feature boys, 10.6 per cent girls, and 12.5 per cent girls and boys together. Moreover, the authors of this study point out that men's and women's roles are unequally distributed: the main characters in 75 per cent of the books studied are boys, as opposed to 25 per cent for girls. Boys have active or entertaining roles: they go fishing or to the beach with their fathers, play football, and fight and claim victory over their enemies; while girls are either nowhere to be seen, or are shown playing with dolls.

The same phenomenon may be observed in an Arabic book for children in the 11-to-13 age-group, where 82 per cent of illustrations represent boys only, as opposed to 18 per cent for girls alone or girls accompanied by boys. Of twenty-four main characters, 84 per cent are boys or men, and 16 per cent women or girls. Although the book glorifies a historical heroine who distinguished herself in battle at the time of the Prophet, the role of women in education is not even mentioned [25].

The effects of sexism on schoolchildren

The fact that sexism exists at school indicates that it is a reflection of society's prejudices, and that it is, therefore, a social institution which serves to strengthen the sexist attitudes towards girls and women that children absorb even before they start school. The role of the school in this respect is emphasized in the guide prepared by Bisaria [5], who observes that sexist stereotypes existing in society are reflected in education curricula and textbooks, which in turn reinforce them, to the detriment of men and women alike.

The author gives the example of the sexist stereotype whereby girls are discouraged from studying technical and scientific subjects, and makes the point that girls' impressions of being second-class citizens are often conveyed by the teachers themselves. By making such comments as: 'You're only a girl', teachers and mothers alike deter girls from specializing in science or technology. Moreover, these girls are influenced by illiterate women who perpetuate the tradition of segregating the sexes, thus considerably narrowing the intellectual horizons of teenage girls. Furthermore, textbooks describe women solely in terms of their role as housewives, in a family context, or, at best, in stereotyped occupations such as nursing and nursery-school teaching. Unfamiliar with the world of technology, most girls choose to enter literary fields, thus perpetuating the sexist stereotype which dictates that technical and scientific studies are a male preserve.

The sexist stereotypes prevailing at school, which have such a disastrous effect on the education choices of girls, are also to be found in France. According to the study conducted by the French section of the World Federation of Teachers' Unions, the virtual absence of girls and women from experimental science textbooks leads girls to contribute very little to discussion in, among others, physics classes [15, p. 23].

Sexism at school and in textbooks not only influences the education and career choices of girls; it also distorts the perception each sex has of the other. A French study [16] reveals that schoolchildren begin assigning sexist stereotypes to the opposite sex at a very early age, particularly where occupations are concerned. The French primary-school boys (8 to 11 years old) who were questioned tended to underestimate the career prospects of girls by limiting their choices to traditionally female jobs which are merely an extension of the domestic roles women play at home (e.g. hospital nurse, nursery nurse, dressmaker, etc.). Girls, on the other hand, expressed the desire to enter not only traditionally female lines of work, but also the professional roles now open to women, such as doctor, journalist and pilot. However, it must be pointed out that these same girls attributed stereotyped career goals to boys of their own age, whom they imagined to be ambitious and eager to land prestigious, well-paid jobs, whereas the boys tended to be less ambitious than the girls thought them to be. So it appears that boys and girls at primary-school level have already internalized sexist stereotypes concerning the opposite sex [16, pp. 140–50].

In Peru, where textbooks develop the image of women no further than the home context and make no mention of their professional activities, young schoolchildren of both sexes learn that such activities are 'less valued and less publicly visible' [21, p. 164].

The Ukrainian study warns against the harm that may be done by the stereotype of inequality presented in writing and illustrations concerning children's games, as these are described in school textbooks. Such a stereotype of inequality can easily expand to include career stereotypes and give rise to stereotyped ideas of men's rights and women's rights:

The child's inner world is shaped in the game. The game is a source of ideas and habits. That is why the problem of presentation of children's games should be reconsidered by writers of children's books. For instance, we find counterproductive the descriptions of delight and rapture some of the writers experience, when they see an 'unusual' girl playing in company with boys the role of the captain of a ship, or an 'unusual' boy rotating the handle of a sewing machine [11, p. 29].

In the United States, the effects of sexist stereotypes instilled by both the society and the school, in pupils of both sexes, have been studied in great detail. One of the most obvious consequences of such stereotyping has been described as girls' 'fear of success'. Baruch [26] studied this phenomenon in 10-year-old American girls, and discovered that such fear is more often experienced by girls than by boys. Fear of success is generally associated with a fear of not being 'feminine', and of not being socially acceptable; success being seen as incompatible with the sexist stereotypes traditionally associated with women. This same study reveals that girls' fear of success increases as they grow older, reaching its highest point at age 15, as a result of rising social pressure to conform [26, p. 199 et seq.].

Similarly, various studies reveal that intelligence tests show a curve that varies according to age and sex. American girls of pre-school age do better in intelligence tests than do boys, but when test results were monitored throughout primary school, it became clear that the boys progressed faster than the girls, and by the first year of secondary education, boys systematically performed better in intelligence tests than girls.

Before starting school, and in their earliest years of schooling, American boys and girls have already internalized career aspirations conforming to traditional stereotypes of feminity and masculinity. Moreover, sexist stereotypes tend to lower the level of creativity in girls, and to develop a fear of success in them at a very early age. Furthermore, by a kind of feedback, these psycho-sociological barriers that are erected in girls' minds by sexist stereotypes, reinforced by school textbooks and children's literature, develop a feeling of inferiority and lowered self-esteem in girls themselves [27, p. 150]. This feeling of inferiority in turn tends to increase girls' fear of success, thus resulting in lower intellectual performance in some fields. The school plays a significant role in generating this feeling of inferiority and self-denigration in American schoolgirls. A study on teacher/pupil relations conducted in the United States revealed that teachers communicate more with boys than with girls (whether praising, criticizing or asking questions), while girls tended to receive disparaging remarks more often. Such behaviour results in boys—who participate more often than girls in classroom discussion, ask more questions, and receive more attention from their teachers—being seen as the more important of the two sexes, while girls are made to feel inferior. Evidence of this is provided in a study carried out in a primary-school class which showed that girls, while showing more ingenuity than boys when experimenting with scientific toys, were considered by boy and girl pupils alike as having performed less well than boys in the exercise, despite the evidence to the contrary [27, pp. 151–2].

The sense of belittlement that girls feel has been examined by Chombart de Lauwe who, when she asked 8- and 9-year-old French schoolchildren which were their favourite peer-group characters in books and in the media, noticed that the boy characters were by far the most popular. Only 15 per cent of the boys admired the girl characters, while 45 per cent of the girls favoured boy characters. Moreover, while '95 per cent of the boys dreamt of becoming one of the boy characters, ... a third of the girls also imagined themselves as being like the male hero' [14, pp. 23–4]. Thus, in France, just as in the United States, the male role is clearly preferred and its female counterpart is considered inferior. This tends to encourage boys to lock themselves into stereotyped, rigid, male roles, while leading girls to reject female characters because children's literature, textbooks and the media portray them as dull, second-rate, subordinate people, totally lacking in social or professional prestige.

Sexist stereotypes inhibit girls from succeeding in scientific fields. In many countries, parents and educators actually discourage girls from going into such fields, reserving these subjects for boys. In fact, children should be urged to be independent, and to use their initiative, if they are to succeed in these fields. However, girls, unlike boys, seldom receive such advice—whether from people around them, or from children's books and textbooks. Quite the opposite: 'intellectual development in girls is stimulated when they are assertive and active, and feel that they are in control of their own actions and the events affecting their lives' [28, p. 133].

Girls' reluctance to enter scientific careers is also influenced by the continued dominance, for example, of men teachers in the sciences (even in primary schools) and of women in the arts, as pointed out by the Commission of European Communities, which also observes that both sexes are influenced in their curricular choices by self-identification with the teachers of different subjects [22].

The Zambian study notes the consequences of sexist education at school: 'male-centred materials make the females ... identify themselves with values which are generally regarded as bad ... it may be argued that education may be seen as a bad thing to them: it portrays them as victims all the time' [20, p. 9], and thereby conditions children to believe that boys are superior to girls.

These analyses point to the conclusion that, if our goal is to eliminate sexism from children's literature and school textbooks—with a view to enabling children of both sexes to develop their full potential—then action must be taken not only in the field of children's literature, but also in all other sectors of the education system.

There must be an end to
stereotypes which imprison men
and women in sex-based roles.
The illustrations reproduced
in this book, sexist and non-sexist,
have been selected either from
textbooks or from booklets aimed
at making educators more aware of
the problem of sexism in schools.

I

Stereotypes

Games

*It starts in childhood . . .
segregation of the sexes*

2

Girl playing with a doll, boy with building blocks.

Girls and boys playing separately at different games.

3

Boy rowing, girl gazing around.

6

4

Girl on foot.

5

Boy cycling.

36

Towards equality of the sexes

8

Girls and boys playing together.

7

9

Girls and boys playing in the same band.

10

11

Girls are doing woodwork, a girl and a boy are sewing.

37

Stereotypes

Household chores

Only mothers and daughters do housework

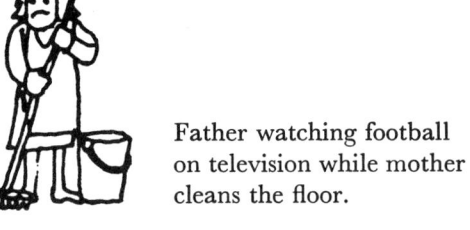

12

It is the girl who has to fetch the water.

13

Father watching football on television while mother cleans the floor.

14

Mother preparing the meal. Father, sitting passively, waiting for it.

15

Mother and daughter laying the table.

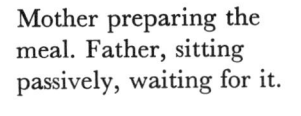

16

It is the girl who has to wait at table.

Towards equality of the sexes

*Children and adults of both sexes
doing household chores*

17

Father laying the table with daughter.

18

19

Boy doing housework.

20

A boy and a girl preparing the meal.

21

Stereotypes

At home

Every member of the household has a clearly defined role . . . according to sex

Father reading, mother knitting.

Father reading aloud, mother darning.

22

23

Towards equality of the sexes

Leisure activities and roles in the family are shared without discrimination

Father and mother looking after their children together.

24

25

Father reading with daughter, mother reading with son.

26

41

Stereotypes

At work

Father earns money to keep his family, mother looks after the children (and does the household chores).

27

Women work only in 'women's jobs':

Typist

28

Auxiliary nurse

29

Cleaning woman

30

42

Towards equality of the sexes

Women and men work together in a laboratory.

Women working in a whole range of different occupations formerly reserved for men.

43

Sources of illustrations

1. Illustration by the Swedish National Committee on Equality between Women and Men.
2, 7, 15, 18, 20, 22, 26. Illustrations published in *Identification and Elimination of Sex Stereotypes in and from School Textbooks—Some Suggestions for Action in the Arab World*, prepared by Julinda Abu Nasr, Irene Lorfing and Jamileh Mikati of the Institute for Women's Studies in the Arab World (Beirut University College), Unesco, Paris, 1983. (ED.84/WS/31.)
3, 23. Illustration from a reader in the Khmer language for the second year of primary schooling published by the Office of the United Nations High Commissioner for Refugees for Khmer refugee children in the Khao I Dang camp in Thailand.
4, 5, 6, 9. Gerda illustrations published in *Le français*, a textbook for the second year of primary schooling, published by Armand Colin, Paris, 1964.
8, 17, 19, 24, 31. Illustrations by Jill Poole, from the *Manuel sur le développement de l'enfant; la vie familiale et la nutrition*, published by the African Training and Research Centre for Women of the United Nations Economic Commission for Africa, Addis-Ababa, 1982.
10. Illustration by Lin Wan-tsouei, from the booklet *Nos petits amis*, published by Éditions en Langues Étrangères, Beijing, 1976.
11. Illustration from the booklet *A Woman in Finland*, published by the Committee on Equality between Men and Women in Finland.
12, 32. Illustrations reproduced by permission of the International Women's Tribune Centre. Artistic director: Anne S. Walker.
13. Illustration from a school textbook published by Det Norske Samlaget, Oslo, Norway, 1983, denouncing traditional sexist stereotypes.
14, 27, 28, 29, 33. Illustrations from the booklet *Zimbabwe Women*, published by the African Training and Research Centre for Women of the United Nations Economic Commission for Africa, Addis-Ababa, 1982.
16. Extract from the ISTRA reading method book *Caroline et Bruno*, published by Éditions André Casteilla, 25 rue Monge, 75005 Paris, 1969.
21, 25, 30. Illustrations by Elisabeth Juell Rasmussen, Kari Grossman and Harald Aadnevik, selected from school textbooks in the 'Likestillinsboka' series published by Cappelen, Oslo, Norway, 1983, 1984.

Part two

Eliminating sexism from children's literature and school textbooks

Introduction

Samples taken from school textbooks and children's literature in different countries reveal that, very often, these publications teach children not only grammar, arithmetic and so forth, but the superiority of one sex over the other; roles of authority, prestige and creativity in these books are assigned to men, while women are invisible, or confined to extremely traditional roles. This habit of teaching so-called 'masculine' and 'feminine' roles to children gives girls a negative self-image and boys a feeling of superiority.

The education goal that Unesco is working to promote throughout the world is, on the contrary, to ensure equality of opportunity for both sexes so that everyone can develop, to the fullest possible extent, his or her potential as a human being. The sexist stereotypes found in school textbooks and children's literature run counter to such a goal. Consequently, one of the most urgent aims of the school should be to become an agent of change with a view to establishing true equality between the sexes. This implies the elimination of sexist stereotypes and, simultaneously, the promotion of a positive image of girls and women, as advocated by Shestakov [3], who points out that achieving true equality between men and women is a twofold process. One half is negative: removing unfavourable stereotypes and prejudice against women from instructional materials; the other is positive: forging a new image of women and increasing their capacity for self-esteem.

Similarly, the Chinese study expresses the hope that 'children's literature and textbooks will play a positive role in promoting equality between men and women [in society], and that the relevant articles of China's Constitution will be further implemented' [10, p. 69].

The Zambian study adopts much the same approach:

One of the formal functions of education is to educate [the] public about how the situation is and how it can be improved. In other words, education can be an agent of change in the society. The books the children read have much to do with the formation of their roles as men, women and workers in the future. In other words, these books help create the adult world. And it is very important that the world in the books conforms to those values which not only reflect the society, but which also show the way the society ought to view the nature of the relationships between boys and girls, men and women [20, p. 23].

Thus, the act of teaching children at school, or adults in lifelong education, should not reinforce discrimination that relegates women to a position of inferiority, but should, rather, be a means of working towards change in this situation of sexual inequality. Consequently, textbooks and children's literature alike take the lead in seeking a solution to this unacceptable state of affairs.

The second part of this study deals with the identification of sexism in textbooks and children's literature, the production of non-sexist children's books and textbooks, and, finally, actions to eliminate sexism within and outside the school system.

3. Identifying sexism in school textbooks and children's literature

Taking as a starting-point the principle that school textbooks and children's literature must not only reflect society, but must also be a factor of change and lay the foundations for the future equality of men and women, two basic criteria can be stated with a view to facilitating the detection of sexism.

First, sexism is present in the text and illustrations of textbooks and children's literature when they depict men and women, boys and girls, in stereotyped activities that do not accurately reflect the diversity of their roles. The first sign of sexism is the refusal to acknowledge social reality and the diversity of situations, resulting in a caricatural depiction of male and female roles. On this point, there seems to be universal agreement.

Second, sexism is also present in textbooks which merely show an existing sexist situation but neither criticize it nor offer any alternative. This amounts to a tacit acceptance of the inequalities and discriminatory behaviour afflicting girls and women in most societies today, and thus serves to strengthen them. This analysis is shared by most of the authors of the national studies.

The Norwegian study, for example, points out that

though there are for instance very few women plumbers, oil workers and professors, it would not be a realistic and well-nuanced presentation *never* to show women in such occupations. ... In other words in our judgement books transmit stereotypes even though the books are in harmony with what the majority of people actually do in real life [12, p. 12].

This study also quotes the view of Skjønsberg [29] on children's literature:

The books may be regarded as realistic in so far as they reflect norms current in large parts of society, but, by limiting themselves to these norms the authors exclude from their readers the knowledge that other patterns of behaviour are possible. By silently accepting the existing state of things without criticism, children's books can be said implicitly to help uphold the traditional sex roles [12, p. 87].

The study conducted by Dunnigan in Quebec echoes this thought:

We do not claim that textbooks ought to hold up a 'carbon copy' of social reality to pupils; they are supposed to be *educational tools*. Young people should be able to find not only a reflection of their environment mirrored therein, but other topics, capable of broadening their intellectual and creative horizons and preparing them for further changes in society. Today, for instance, even though only 10 per cent of Canada's doctors are women, there is no reason to regard this figure as an ultimate ceiling. Textbooks should also show men as nurses, even if there are very few male nurses to date. The aim here is to suggest new career possibilities, which may not have been available to the previous generation, but which certainly exist for young people nowadays [2, p. 176].

The author of the guide for Asia and the Pacific adds that, in the fight against sexism, the mere elimination from textbooks of stereotyped women's and men's roles is not enough, and that a more positive approach must be taken by promoting non-traditional roles for men and women, which are not yet prevalent in Indian society. Some examples of these roles are: women decision-makers, women engineers or mathematicians, sensitive male poets, writers or painters, women athletes, hardy women in rural settings, brave women in peace and war, and women entrepreneurs in the industrial sector [5, p. 53].

From the opinions expressed by the authors of the national studies, it is apparent that two categories of sexism exist: first, explicit sexism, when children's literature and textbooks depict men, women, boys and girls exclusively in fixed, stereotyped conventional roles, without taking into account the diversity to be found in the real world; and second, implicit, or latent, sexism, when these texts describe a real society where women and girls are treated as inferior to men and boys, and make no attempt to challenge this alleged inferiority or to introduce children to situations (however rare they still may be) where women and girls prove that they are equal to men and boys.

Analytical checklist for the identification of sexism

The analytical approach as outlined below may be used by any person or organization desiring to identify sexism in the text and illustrations of a particular textbook, children's novel or other publication. This checklist can be divided into three parts, varying according to the content of the work under consideration:

Quantitative analysis of content: a statistical and comparative evaluation of the number of male and female characters featuring in the titles, texts and illustrations of children's literature and textbooks.

Qualitative analysis of content: a statistical comparison of the characteristics attributed to male and female characters featuring in the titles, texts and illustrations of children's literature and textbooks.

Analysis of sexism inherent in the language: a study of the use of vocabulary, grammatical structure and insinuations.

By taking all three aspects of sexism into consideration, this analysis should result in a thorough, if not exhaustive, evaluation of the sexism occurring in any kind of publication.

Quantitative analysis of content

The analysis of sexism contained in books and textbooks should always be based on statistics comparing the number of male and female characters who appear both in the body of the text and its illustrations. Dunnigan, who in 1974/75 conducted a survey of 225 primary- and secondary-school textbooks in Quebec, found that, of 24,000 male and female characters, there were more than twice as many men as women (68 per cent men as opposed to 32 per cent women). This in itself is an indication of sexism, since in virtually all societies, the number of women is equal, or even superior, to that of men. Women's absence from, or under-representation in, books and textbooks is a clear indication of the inferior position to which women are relegated in society, and helps to aggravate the situation still further. Such under-representation is in itself a sexist stereotype.

A further step can be taken in this analysis by distinguishing between main and supporting characters; the main character being the one who plays the central role in the story (including the title and illustrations) or in the body of the textbook, while the supporting role is subordinate to the main character. The Quebec study revealed that out of 100 main character roles, 72 per cent are played by men or boys, while only 28 per cent are played by women or girls. Dunnigan concludes from this first part of the analysis that Quebec textbooks are steeped in sexist stereotypes, in that men are twice as much in evidence as women and the main characters in almost three-quarters of the texts are men.

Qualitative analysis of content

According to the analytical approach used in the Quebec study, the characteristics attributed to male and female characters in books or textbooks fall into three categories [2, p. 5]: social references, activities, and social and emotional behaviour of the characters. Before this method is applied, two basic principles should be adopted.

First, that a textbook or children's book cannot be labelled sexist if, throughout the text and illustrations, only one stereotyped role is attributed to a single male or female character. For sexism to exist, there must be a repetition of stereotypes, in either illustrations or texts. Obviously, the case of a single illustration or text commending the subservience or inferiority of women or girls will be an exception to this rule.

Second, the analytical unit of sexism is the male or female character, whether he or she be represented in human form (child, adult, elderly person), or as a male or female animal. The Zambian study detected sexism in one story, among others, in a third-grade textbook, where both protagonists were animals (a dog as a male symbol and a goat as a female symbol). The story shows the goat being tricked by the dog, and the author concludes that it is sexist because by and large the textbook portrays the male as clever, and the female as stupid [20, p. 6].

The traits attributed to male and female characters identified in the Quebec study are criteria which can be used to detect sexism in children's literature and textbooks and to gauge its extent and seriousness. We have chosen to adopt these three basic criteria, adding a few categories of our own.

ANALYSIS OF SEXISM
IN THE SOCIAL REFERENCES
TO MALE AND FEMALE CHARACTERS,
IN BOTH TEXTS AND ILLUSTRATIONS

The expression 'social reference' here refers to the static traits attributed to male and female characters in textbooks and children's literature. We must be careful to distinguish social references from the activities and behavioural roles of the characters: social references involve the character's marital and family status, level of employment, life-style and occupation.

Marital status

Sexist stereotypes appear in textbooks and children's books which portray men and women differently in terms of their marital status. For example, a textbook which depicts most women as married, whereas most men are not so described, conveys a sexist stereotype in so far as it would have children believe that women's status is linked to marriage, while men are independent. Social reality, however, indicates that not only are there approximately as many married men as women, but that there is a large percentage of men and women who are unmarried or no longer married: single people, widowers/widows, those who are divorced, separated, or, in the case of some people, repudiated. In the industrialized countries, there are more widows than widowers, owing to women's longer life expectancy. It is estimated that, worldwide, one household in three is headed by a woman. Children's literature and textbooks never seem to include such families, choosing instead to make the man the head of the household, in keeping with the traditional sexist stereotype. Not only does this approach turn a blind eye to social reality, but it ignores the existence of single women who, breaking with traditional standards, assume responsibility for single-parent families.

Family status

The frequent definition of women characters solely in terms of their role in the family (usually as mothers), while men characters are only occasionally portrayed as fathers, is another indicator of sexism. In real life, both men and women are called upon to fulfil their roles as parents, even though men often prefer to leave the trouble of raising and educating children to women. Moreover, the depiction of women as mothers is tantamount to denying human worth to those women who find fulfilment outside of motherhood, such as those who take on social, professional or political responsibilities, or who have two roles, one in the family and one outside the home.

Level of employment

The 1971 Canadian census found that women constitute over one-third of the working population in Canada (35 per cent); however, working women in the 225 textbooks examined in the Quebec study make up only 10 per cent of all persons of both sexes shown as having an occupation. This glaring misrepresentation means that children are led to believe that the woman's place is in the home, while that of the man is at work [2, p. 35].

Another example arises in a study of 134 textbooks in use in the state of New Jersey, United States, which reveals that men therein are portrayed as having access to 147 different occupations, whereas women have access to only 25 [30, p. 119].

The analysis of textbooks used in Quebec schools reveals that over 50 per cent of all adults are pictured at their place of work, but that only 17 per cent of women are so portrayed. Conversely, only 6.6 per cent of men are shown at home, compared with 26 per cent of women [2, p. 47]. The same discrepancy is found between boys and girls, boys being shown more often at school and outdoors than girls.

Occupation

The approach used for analysing social references to characters in texts and illustrations should not confine itself to determining whether or not characters have an occupation. It is also important to ascertain if the occupations carry with them implicit sexist stereotypes. When women's occupations are shown to be an extension of women's traditional domestic roles (e.g. hospital nurse, nursery nurse, dressmaker, teacher of young children, hairdresser), or when the book neglects to show any other occupations held by women in society today (e.g. doctor, lawyer, bus-driver, works supervisor, factory manager, horticulturist, physicist), we can claim that such a textbook contains sexist stereotypes. By the same token, textbooks portraying only men in occupations that carry prestige or authority—contradicting what children see in the real world—can also be dubbed sexist.

ANALYSIS OF SEXISM IN THE ACTIVITIES OF MALE AND FEMALE CHARACTERS

For the sake of clarity, it is proposed to divide the activities allotted to male and female characters into five categories: domestic tasks carried out in the home; contributing to the education of children; professional activities; political or social activities; and leisure activities (sport, art, hobbies, etc.).

Analysis of the respective roles played by men, women, boys and girls in these activities will reveal any sexism that is present.

Domestic tasks carried out in the home

This category includes housekeeping activities (tidying up, cleaning, sewing, etc.), as well as cooking and related activities (shopping, food preparation, etc.). For the developing countries, the tasks of water-carrying and wood-gathering must also be added. The sexist stereotypes are those texts and illustrations which show such tasks as being the domain of women and girls alone, while men and boys are systematically excused from them [2, pp. 64, 69]. In Quebec textbooks, 85 per cent of household chores are performed by women or girls, but only 17 per cent by men or boys. Where cooking is concerned, these figures change slightly, with 77 per cent of tasks performed by women and 25 per cent by men.

Contributing to the education of children

This category concerns adult/child relationships, their frequency and their nature [2, p. 53]. Quebec textbooks show many more women than men in contact with children, which constitutes a stereotype, as it assigns women a monopoly of the care of young children. Other stereotypes emerge when this relationship is scrutinized more closely: while women are shown as attending to the material and emotional well-being of their children (feeding, washing, dressing, encouraging, reassuring, comforting, etc.), men are shown in roles of authority (answering children's questions, introducing them to new things, helping them to solve problems, etc.).

Professional activities

While social references to employment or careers are confined to observing how many adults of both sexes have a paid job and into what occupational category that job falls, the 'professional activities' indicator refers more specifically to men or women characters shown acting in a professional capacity (e.g. a doctor treating a patient, or a teacher giving a lesson). Sexist stereotypes can be detected when the professional activities of women and men are broken down respectively into roles of 'doing the work' and 'giving the orders'. The fact that most women are described as employees carrying out orders, engaging in repetitive work and/or tasks requiring little initiative, while men are nearly always shown in roles of authority, carrying out non-repetitive jobs requiring initiative and creativity, is an indication that the texts of such books convey sexist stereotypes; for in fact there are women who, in whatever professional field, show authority, initiative and creativity, just as there are men who exhibit none of these qualities.

Political or social activities

This category includes any activity involving political or social responsibilities in a wider context than the family or a job: at the local or national levels, in the public sector, or in a national or international organization (mayor of a town, for instance, or head of a club or social, artistic, cultural or sporting association). Using this indicator as a starting point, it is easy to detect the presence of sexist stereotypes. And, since virtually all political and social roles described in textbooks are allocated to male characters, such books stand accused of conveying sexist prejudice; for today, as in the past, women perform political and social functions that require authority, responsibility and a spirit of initiative.

Leisure activities

In the area of hobbies, sports, artistic activities, etc., it is also easy to detect sexist stereotypes. In order to do this different evaluation criteria can be adopted applicable to all areas touching on leisure activities: the criterion of activity and creativity as opposed to passiveness and lack of creativity; and the criterion of autonomy as opposed to heteronomy [2, p. 75].

Hobbies and crafts

Non-professional activities such as woodworking, sculpture, painting, pottery, sewing, etc., should be examined with a view to determining whether they require creativity or initiative on the part of those men, women, boys and girls who engage in them. If such activities are depicted as lacking in initiative and independence when women perform them, while these qualities are attributed to boys and men, the textbook can be said to contain sexist stereotypes.

Artistic activities

If in activities such as singing, dance, music, theatre, entertainment, etc., girls and women are shown as passive spectators while boys and men are seen as actively engaged, sexism can be said to be present.

Games

Using the example of the Ukrainian study [11], it was observed above that close attention must be paid to sexist stereotypes which describe as 'exceptional' a girl playing the 'gang leader', or a boy using a sewing machine, for example. It seems obvious that boys and girls should be represented in texts and illustrations alike as being able to participate in so-called boys' and girls' games, bringing to them the same amounts of initiative and daring. Sexism is thus discernible when texts and illustrations depict boys' games as full of daring, excitement and initiative, while qualifying girls' games in terms of timidity, repetition, passivity and lack of initiative. The Zambian study brands two first-grade textbooks as sexist, as they show a boy playing football, while a girl looks on passively, content to applaud the exploits of her male playmate [20, p. 4].

Exploration and adventure

As described in textbooks, these activities are sexist in so far as they are attributed exclusively to boys and men, whereas in fact there have been women explorers and adventurers throughout history, such as female pirates, mountaineers in the Himalayas, etc.

Sport

The Kuwaiti study [25] points out that only male sports champions are mentioned in a social science textbook, while mention is never made of female champions. Quebec textbooks, too, exhibit this kind of sexism, for in 90 per cent of all books analysed, sports activities are performed by men or boys, and in only 10 per cent by women [2, p. 76]. Yet in Canada, as in other countries, there are many outstanding female athletes, some of them Olympic medal winners.

ANALYSIS OF SEXISM IN THE SOCIAL AND EMOTIONAL BEHAVIOUR OF MALE AND FEMALE CHARACTERS

Following Dunnigan's Canadian example, social and emotional behaviour can be classified into three categories: positive versus negative emotions; resistance to social pressure versus dependence and docility; and weakness of character (cowardice, confusion, dependence, helplessness, etc.) versus strength of character (courage, tenacity, etc.) [2, p. 25].

Positive or negative emotions

It is easy to understand how texts and illustrations which depict girls and women as affectionate or overly emotional, and boys and men as aggressive, violent, combative and insensitive, are sexist, as they convey stereotypes which caricature male and female characters in a manner that reflects conventional prejudices.

Resistance to social pressure

A text's depiction of the way in which an individual behaves (man or woman, boy or girl) when faced with standards, social pressure and authority, can be an accurate indicator of the presence of sexist stereotypes, if, for example, independence from and resistance to social pressure are shown as being characteristic of one sex, while the other is described as docile, resigned and always yielding to authority and social pressure.

Weakness and strength of character

Weakness of character, according to the research approach adopted by Dunnigan, appears in texts in the form of cowardice, confusion, dependence, helplessness and evasiveness, while strength of character is expressed in bravery, level-headedness, an ability to give orders and a sense of responsibility. Here again, a good indicator of sexist stereotypes is the way in which weaknesses and strengths of character are divided between male and female characters. Using this indicator, her analysis revealed that Quebec textbooks are sexist, since in a hundred situations requiring strength of character, 90 per cent depicted boys and men and only 10 per cent girls and women [2, p. 97]. Indeed, textbooks in Quebec seem to have been written not only for the purpose of teaching arithmetic and grammar, but also in order to promote the idea that social independence and strength of character are male-specific qualities.

Comparative analysis of the character traits attributed to males and females (both adults and children) in texts and illustrations of textbooks and children's literature seems particularly appropriate for the identification of sexist stereotypes.

Analysis of sexism inherent in the language

Sexism in textbooks and children's literature can also manifest itself in the choice of vocabulary, in the use of grammar, and in supposedly innocuous insinuations which conceal a sexist message.

SEXISM IN VOCABULARY

The excessive use of the masculine gender to denote all individuals, male and female, making up the human race leads to a denigration of women by making them invisible. How can a young child be expected not to scorn women, or not to consider them inferior, when a masculine noun (i.e. 'man' in English) is used to refer not only to men, but to women as well? Thus, when in French the expression *'les droits de l'homme'* (the rights of man) is used to denote human rights, children conclude that the rights of women are somehow not included in human rights. To say that 'all men are created equal' is to tell the child that women are not equal to men. Examples of this linguistic bias are endless.

The predominant number of male characters over female characters becomes sharply apparent when we analyse the frequency, not of characters, but of the words (nouns and pronouns) used in texts to designate each sex. With this in mind, the Norwegian study [12, p. 40] examined three history textbooks, counting the number of nouns and pronouns that were used to denote male and female characters. Their findings reveal a marked preponderance of masculine nouns and pronouns over their feminine equivalents, as indicated in Table 1.

TABLE 1. Words designating males and females

	Class 4 Male	Class 4 Female	Class 7 Male	Class 7 Female
Number of times mentioned	565	180	399	45
As a percentage	78	22	90	10

Some languages can also be criticized for using masculine words to denote functions and occupations that can be indiscriminately male or female. In English, for example, the word 'chairman' is often used instead of 'chairperson' and 'postman' instead of 'mail carrier', etc. The use of masculine nouns to designate functions or occupations that can be performed by either men or women can lead the child to think that such activities are for men only.

Moreover, there are a number of abstract nouns that are commonly used to describe humanity as a whole, or a social group, which lead children to believe either that women should not be mentioned precisely because they are women, or that women have had little influence throughout history. For example, in English, the words 'mankind', 'forefathers' and the 'average man' are used to refer to both sexes.

SEXISM IN GRAMMAR

The French and Spanish languages are sexist as a result of their grammatical rules, which stipulate that when there are two nouns, one masculine and the other feminine, then the corresponding adjectives and pronouns must be in the masculine plural. This grammatical rule teaches the child a sexist message that men take precedence over women. Similarly, the Kuwaiti study notes that in that country's textbooks, masculine grammatical forms are used when both men and women are intended [25].

INSINUATIONS

Insinuations are a carefully camouflaged form of sexism. They serve to attribute non-conventional roles to one sex as if such roles were the exclusive property of one sex instead of both. Unesco's suggestions for research in the study of stereotypes concentrates on this aspect of insinuations in textbook and literature content: 'Content/slurs . . . concern words, statements, modifiers, innuendoes, etc., in texts or illustrations which are sexist (i.e. this girl runs and jumps like a boy; he is as weak as a girl, etc.).'[1] Similarly, to say that a woman has succeeded 'even though she's a woman' is a sexist remark, as is 'she's as fast as a boy', as this implies that it is normal for boys to run quickly, but unusual for girls. The English language once again proves sexist when it describes a girl who runs, climbs trees, plays football, etc., as a 'tomboy'; that is, she engages in activities that are supposedly reserved for boys.

Conversely, to say of a boy who plays with a doll or a teddy bear that he is playing 'girls' games' is a sexist stereotype, as it means that showing tenderness towards a doll or a stuffed animal is an emotional display only suitable for girls. Just as girls have the right to develop their physical capacities to the same extent as boys in exercise, games and sport, so boys have the right to develop their emotional potential in cuddling a doll or teddy bear.

To say that a girl is acting like a boy or that a boy is acting like a girl amounts to dividing the whole range of human activities, games and sports into two different categories, one of which is the exclusive domain of boys and hence forbidden to girls, and vice versa. At the same time, we have seen that no aspect of human potential, whether it involves intelligence, emotion or activity, can be denied to a human being on the basis of his or her sex. Choices must be made in the light of the aspirations and preferences of those concerned, and not on the basis of sexist stereotypes.

Outline for a simplified sexist stereotypes checklist

The foregoing observations, which can be used as a detailed guide to the examination of sexist stereotypes in textbooks, may be summarized in the form of a checklist (Table 2), which is based on the outline

1. See Appendix 1, page 87.

TABLE 2. Outline for a simplified sexist stereotype checklist for children's literature and textbooks

1. Comparative analysis of the number of male and female references

		Women / Girls	Men / Boys	Animals F. M.
Number of hes/shes[1]	titles: texts: illustrations:			
Number of girls/boys	titles: texts: illustrations:			
Number of women/men	titles: texts: illustrations:			

2. Comparative analysis of male and female activities[2]

Conventional activities (CA)[3]
Non-conventional activities (NCA)[4]

Specify:

Activities in the family and at school
(a) conventional
(b) non-conventional
Occupational activities
(a) conventional
(b) non-conventional
Political and social activities
(a) conventional
(b) non-conventional
Other activities (leisure, sport, games, etc.)
(a) conventional
(b) non-conventional

3. Comparative analysis of male and female character traits

Conventional traits (CT)
Non-conventional traits (NCT)

1. The 'hes' and 'shes' are counted only when they refer to living beings (humans, animals) and not to inanimate objects.
2. Obviously, the classification of 'conventional' and 'non-conventional' activities may vary from country to country. Users of this checklist should take such variations into account.
3. The total number of conventional activities (CA) may be obtained by adding together the conventional activities (a) for each sex in each category of activities listed under the heading 'Specify'.
4. The total number of non-conventional activities (NCA) can be obtained by adding together the non-conventional activities (b) for each sex in each category of activities listed under the heading 'Specify'.

proposed in the Norwegian study [12, p. 102]. The Norwegian identification checklist makes provision for a comparative analysis of the number of female and male characters and their respective activities and personality traits.

The outline in Table 2 has the advantage of breaking down sexist stereotypes in several different ways: according to the numerical importance of male and female characters and according to the distribution by sex of activities and character traits. Moreover, we can distinguish these three areas of analysis by using as a basis the title, the text or the illustrations of a book or textbook. The outline thus makes it possible to ascertain the exact area of sexist stereotype, since a book or textbook may be sexist in one area and not in another—sexist in female images but not in male, sexist in title and illustrations but not in the body of the text. For example, there may be a children's grammar book or reader which, while representing men and women more or less equally in conventional and non-conventional professional activities, continues to portray men and women through conventional stereotypes in family life, with household, domestic and education tasks falling to women and girls, while men and boys are excused from such work. It is thus possible to distinguish between and comprehend different degrees of sexism from one publication to another, and from one textbook to another, although in Chapters 1 and 2 of this study we have shown that the different kinds of sexist stereotypes tend to be found together in all fields.

The sexism in a publication or textbook does not need to occur in all three categories of this checklist in order for the book to be described as sexist. Table 3 can be used to identify the areas in which a textbook or children's book is sexist.

Being careful to avoid too mechanical an interpretation, we can read Table 3 as follows:

1. $Mn = Fn$ means that the number of masculine and feminine words (nouns, pronouns, names of people or animals in the relevant category, title, text

TABLE 3. Identification of sexism in textbooks after application of the checklist

		Sexism	No sexism
1. Comparison of masculine nouns (Mn) and feminine nouns (Fn): pronouns, characters, animals	Titles	$Mn > Fn$	$Mn = Fn$
	Texts	$Mn > Fn$	$Mn = Fn$
	Illustrations	$Mn > Fn$	$Mn = Fn$
2. Comparison of conventional activities (CA) and non-conventional activities (NCA):			
Analysis of female characters	Titles	$CA > NCA$	$CA = NCA$
	Texts	$CA > NCA$	$CA = NCA$
	Illustrations	$CA > NCA$	$CA = NCA$
Analysis of male characters	Titles	$CA > NCA$	$CA = NCA$
	Texts	$CA > NCA$	$CA = NCA$
	Illustrations	$CA > NCA$	$CA = NCA$
3. Comparison of conventional character traits (CT) and non-conventional character traits (NCT):			
Analysis of female characters	Titles	$CT > NCT$	$CT = NCT$
	Texts	$CT > NCT$	$CT = NCT$
	Illustrations	$CT > NCT$	$CT = NCT$
Analysis of male characters	Titles	$CT > NCT$	$CT = NCT$
	Texts	$CT > NCT$	$CT = NCT$
	Illustrations	$CT > NCT$	$CT = NCT$

or illustration) in a publication, textbook or a series of publications or textbooks, is equal, and that therefore there is no sexism, quantitatively speaking. If, on the other hand, the number of masculine words is higher than the number of feminine words (Mn > Fn), sexism is present.

2. CA = NCA means that the number of conventional activities attributed to girls is equal to the number of non-conventional activities, and we can say that in the category concerned (title, text or illustration) there is no sexism. If, on the other hand, conventional activities of girls are more frequently cited than non-conventional activities (CA > NCA), sexism is present. The same analysis will apply to boys.

3. CT = NCT means that in the personality traits attributed to girls, the numbers of conventional and non-conventional traits are equal; thus there is no sexism. If, on the other hand, the number of conventional traits is higher than that of non-conventional traits (CT > NCT), sexism is present. The same analysis will apply to boys.

As we have said before, it is difficult to apply this table systematically in all areas mentioned. Indeed, it is Utopian to posit a publication whose texts systematically contain an equal number of masculine and feminine nouns and pronouns. On the other hand, more care should be taken over illustrations, given their influence on young children's imaginations. The attribution of character traits and conventional or non-conventional activities to both sexes should not deviate by more than 10 to 20 per cent from the ideal distribution of 50 per cent. However, even if this equal balance is disturbed, compensatory measures can be taken, for example, if fewer women than men appear in the text, they can be given more emphasis qualitatively (i.e. described as having more non-conventional character traits and activities than men).

Whatever the solution adopted, the elimination of sexism from texts and illustrations in children's literature and textbooks is incompatible, either with the total absence or under-representation of women and girls, or with their relegation to activities and behaviour patterns considered to be negative or inferior.

Outline for a simplified sexist occupational activities checklist

A second checklist can be used to analyse sexism in the occupations of female and male characters. This checklist (page 90) has been compiled from the suggestions for research prepared by Unesco in the framework of the series of national studies of men and women in school textbooks and children's literature. Conventional occupations of men and women can be easily identified by this means, so that, for example, if most women are shown as having so-called 'female' occupations instead of having occupations equally divided between both columns, the publication or textbook can be called sexist. The same criterion can be used for male occupations. Conversely, if the occupations held by women in a children's book or a textbook are divided more or less equally between the two columns of the sex-stereotyped occupations table, we can say that such a publication is not sexist in its portrayal of women's occupations.

Latent sexism in social references and in the activities of male and female characters

We have already seen that one, very important, aspect of latent sexism is justification of the subordinate position of women and girls in relation to men and boys. Such justification is not made explicit, but consists rather in neglecting to show any alternative, or to propose a solution likely to improve this situation or to eliminate women's subordinate role. Thus, depicting women as wives and mothers only, without showing them independently from husband and children, is tantamount to informing children in a veiled way that women exist only by virtue of their role as wives dependent on husbands, or subordinate to children's needs.

Another form of latent sexism is the refusal to portray all aspects of social reality; as a result, textbooks' depiction of reality is slanted, causing children to form a distorted image of the real world. Thus, despite the set of recommendations sent to its authors by a major French publishing firm, Fernand Nathan,[1] a sexist textbook on twentieth-century literature was published in Paris in 1983. The choice of texts by the three authors of this work clearly reveals that they underestimate or ignore altogether the work of women writers; and of the few women writers chosen, they emphasize militant writing rather than fiction or literary criticism. For example, the textbook quotes only twenty lines from Simone de Beauvoir's *The Second Sex*, in which she criticizes the work of Montherlant, concentrating instead on her feminist writings, not her novels, and on the feminist movement rather than any other social movement.

Such omissions lead students of both sexes to form an erroneous concept of twentieth-century literature, of the rightful place of women writers therein, and of what women have to say in their literary works.

---

1. See Appendix 3, page 98.

4. Producing non-sexist children's literature and school textbooks

It is quite feasible, as outlined above, to detect sexism in a children's book or school textbook by using a checklist for the identification of sex stereotypes. In producing a non-sexist book or textbook, therefore, one must avoid anything that has been condemned as sexist prejudice. A handbook for the purpose may be of assistance to authors and illustrators wishing to produce such non-sexist material.

In 1972, in response to initiatives by American feminists, a major American publisher, McGraw-Hill, drew up a set of guidelines for equal treatment of the sexes in school textbooks to be used by authors of children's books and textbooks published by that firm.[1] In France, Fernand Nathan, a publisher of children's literature and school textbooks, also made recommendations to be followed by authors and illustrators.[2]

The following brief guidelines for the production of non-sexist publications make no claim to be either restrictive or exhaustive. Readers may supplement them if they so wish by referring to the documents prepared by McGraw-Hill and Fernand Nathan.

Brief guidelines for the production of non-sexist publications

Equitable ratio of female to male characters

The ratio of female to male characters should be equitable in all publications, in the title and the body of the text, and in any quotations and illustrations. In choosing personal pronouns and collective nouns, a constant effort should be made to avoid giving precedence to one sex over the other.

Equitable distribution of roles between women and men

IN THE FAMILY

A non-sexist publication will show equal numbers of girls and boys performing household tasks and looking after younger brothers and sisters, and equal numbers of women and men doing domestic chores, teaching and looking after the children or earning the family living. Both girls and boys will have dolls and play at tea parties, and will take part in ball games, electronic games, tree-climbing, sewing, gardening, knitting, and so on.

The mother and father should be portrayed as parents on an equal footing, with the same responsibilities, who talk things over together before making joint decisions. The traditional image of the resigned wife passively awaiting her husband's decision must disappear. If one of the parents has to stay at home to look after the children, it will be either the mother or the father. Instead of giving the impression that the family suffers when the mother has a job outside the home, the wife's work should be placed on a par with that of her husband, and the point should be made that the family as a whole can only benefit from the fact that both parents go out to work. Many sociological studies have now con-

1. See Appendix 2, page 92.
2. See Appendix 3, page 98.

cluded that the impact on children of having a mother employed outside the home is decidedly beneficial.

Moreover, instead of representing only traditional and/or complete families consisting of father, mother and children, it should be made clear that there are various possible types of family, ranging from the extended family, in which the couple and the children live together with grandparents, collateral relatives and non-relatives, to single-parent families, 80 per cent of which are run by women, whose status is that of 'head of the household'. In the world as a whole, 33 per cent of households are actually run by women, and a much larger percentage of families or households depend on women's work for their survival.

Writers and illustrators should avoid portraying women solely as wives or mothers, since women, like men, can lead a bona fide existence as unmarried or childless individuals. Children in illustrations should be shown as equally close to, and just as often in the company of, their father as their mother, to avoid suggesting to young people that women have the monopoly of child-raising and child care. In addition, equal numbers of fathers and mothers, husbands and wives, should be shown working in the kitchen, doing odd mechanical or repair jobs, cleaning, washing, ironing, etc., since there is no household or domestic chore that cannot be done by either sex. In short, activities carried out in the family at all stages of human life (childhood, adolescence, adulthood, old age) will be rated equally highly for the two sexes.

IN SCHOOL LIFE

Parents, teachers at all levels and other adults of both sexes should be shown attaching the same importance to girls' and boys' teaching and vocational training. In non-sexist publications, boys will do equally well in languages and literature, girls in mathematics and science. There will be descriptions of boys aspiring to enter traditionally female careers and girls interested in traditionally male careers.

There will be an equal percentage of headmasters and headmistresses and of male and female school inspectors, all of them doing their job equally efficiently. Illustrations of playgrounds or sports fields will no longer show girls looking on in passive admiration as boys play ball or exert themselves. Girls will be shown instead playing all kinds of games, which may or may not be mixed, and they will be just as active, capable, agile and adventurous as the boys. 'Leadership' in games will be shared equally between the two sexes.

IN WORKING LIFE

Just like educational and domestic activities, working life should also be equally divided between the two sexes. In other words, in non-sexist publications we should not find only men going out to work and only women staying at home, but both women and men equally represented in domestic and vocational roles. Furthermore, women and men will not be confined to conventional, traditional female or male occupations. For example, there will be women engineers, aeronauts, pilots, doctors, surgeons, architects, mathematicians, electricians and highly skilled workers, and male nurses, typists, unskilled workers and grocery shop assistants. Competence and professionalism, ambition, dedication, eagerness to learn, to be useful in one's career, to better oneself, and to take part in scientific discovery or artistic creation will be encountered in equal proportions in the two sexes, as will negative characteristics (incompetence, lack of professionalism, lack of interest in one's work, in learning new things, in being useful, in bettering oneself or in raising one's general career status). High-ranking posts will also be distributed equitably between women and men; company directors, directors of hospitals, schools, research laboratories, industrial and commercial enterprises, banks, etc., will no longer be exclusively male; women will also be shown as perfectly capable of holding positions of management, responsibility and authority. The negative or positive characteristics associated with the exercise of such functions will be shared equally between the two sexes, women being endowed with resourcefulness, abilities and skills to the same extent as men in the same jobs.

Children will thus no longer be tempted to put an exclusive premium on male skills and professional standing, while undervaluing the role of working women, whose competence, professional responsibility and wide range of qualifications are generally ignored in sexist writings and illustrations. Women's merits and qualifications will as a result be explicitly mentioned, recognized and respected by the children.

IN SOCIAL AND POLITICAL ROLES

In social roles other than those that are vocational, women and men should be given equal prominence, not only quantitatively but also qualitatively. Women in non-sexist publications will be shown discharging political and social functions at all levels (village, district, region, nation, international, intergovernmental and non-governmental organizations) with the same competence, authority and spirit of initiative as their male colleagues. The negative characteristics attributed to particular activities will not reflect on women alone, but also on men in the same proportion. As stressed in the Norwegian study [12], the latest research findings on women (in the social sciences, history and other fields) must be used in order to show women in as good a light as men. The Kuwaiti study [25] suggests, moreover, that history books should not focus on outstanding representatives of one sex only. In today's world, although there are fewer female than male heads of government, women are as numerous as men in performing social functions that are essential to society's survival (many women set up associations to fight for the cause of peace, to persuade governments to choose a development model based on principles of equity, the preservation of nature and the human species, etc.). All these activities, frequently 'initiated' by women, are still ignored, discounted or held in low esteem by the political parties; they must now, therefore, be appreciated at their true worth in children's literature and school textbooks.

Fields of activity or situations (in the family, in occupations, in political or social contexts, etc.) in which only one sex shows initiative, intelligence and dedication are to be avoided. Women showing intelligence, maturity and initiative should not be portrayed solely in family life, while men with the same qualities are shown in political, social or cultural and professional contexts. Intellectual, emotional and volitional qualities (or their negative counterparts) should be shared equally between the sexes in all areas of family, vocational, social and political life. As regards domestic chores, women as well as men may be shown as either expert or clumsy, and the same rule applies to professional and political life.

Instead of viewing the family as the preserve of women as wives and mothers, and professional, social and political life as that of men, children will realize that there are no domains reserved for one sex and that women are just as capable as men of succeeding in any branch of society.

Equitable distribution of good and bad qualities between the sexes

Girls, boys, women and men must be assigned the same proportion of positive or negative psychological or physical characteristics, so as to avoid sex stereotyping through continual attribution of the same negative or positive characteristics to one sex. Both girls and boys in non-sexist publications will be described either as obedient and submissive to parents and adults or as disobedient, independent or rebellious.

PHYSICAL APPEARANCE AND CLOTHING

Girls and women will no longer be depicted in narratives, titles or illustrations in submissive or passive attitudes or in conventional dress, indicating a state of dependence and the correspondingly conventional role expected of representatives of the female sex. For example, both men and women will be shown suitably dressed for the performance of household chores, so that children do not get the impression that women belong in the kitchen or have the monopoly of housework. Just as many girls as boys will be shown untidily dressed, since all children, regardless of sex, have the right to climb trees, ride bicycles, play football and soil their clothes while playing. Moreover, coquettish and well-groomed boys and men will exist alongside their female counterparts. There must be an end to the stereotyping of girls and women through value judgements based solely on appearance and coquetry, since this is basically a way of reducing their status to that of a sex object. To sum up, casual clothing, elegance, coquetry and the many varieties of dress and hairstyle will be distributed equally between the two sexes.

INTELLECTUAL ABILITIES AND DISABILITIES

Equal numbers of girls and boys should be shown as intelligent, competent, brilliant, imaginative, creative and good at mathematics, science of the arts; and, conversely, lacking in intelligence, incompetent, dull, unimaginative or uncreative and poor at mathematics, science or the arts. Thus, all intellectual characteristics, both negative and positive, generally attributed to women in some cases and to men in others, will be shared evenly between the two sexes.

EMOTIONAL VIRTUES AND VICES

A serious effort must be made to depict equal numbers of girls and boys, women and men as being capable of maturity, dedication, consideration for others, self-control, gentleness, kindness and objectivity; or, alternatively, as displaying immaturity, egoism, lack of consideration for others, emotionalism, brutality, hard-heartedness and subjectivity.

VOLITIONAL MERITS AND DEMERITS

Equal numbers of girls, boys, women and men should be described as active, independent, intrepid, self-confident, resolute, persevering, courageous and heroic; or, on the contrary, as passive, dependent, timorous, diffident, indecisive, irresolute, fearful and cowardly.

These character traits, both negative and positive, will be meted out in equal proportions to the two sexes, whatever the field concerned: family, society, education, career, social life, leisure, sport, politics, etc.

Avoiding sexism in vocabulary, grammar and syntax

VOCABULARY

Acknowledging the sexism implicit in the use of the Arabic term for 'mankind', the Kuwaiti study [25] suggests adding to that concept the phrase 'women and men' so as not to insinuate that humanity consists solely of the male sex. Likewise, the term 'man' in English used to designate humanity tends to leave the female sex out of account, diminishing its value in the eyes of children of both sexes. It is therefore more fitting to use a term representing both sexes indiscriminately ('humanity' or 'humankind', for example) or to refer explicitly in speech and writing to 'women *and* men'. To the same end, the French term *les droits de l'homme* (human rights) will be replaced in non-sexist publications by *les droits des humains*. In English, the sexist terms 'mankind', 'forefathers', 'average man' will be replaced by neutral concepts ('chairperson' instead of 'chairman', for example), or both sexes will be mentioned (for example, 'mankind and womankind', 'forefathers and foremothers', 'average man and average women', etc.).

Names of occupations, which are very frequently linked to the male sex, should be replaced by sexually neutral nouns to make it clear to children that these jobs are open to both sexes. This can be done either by putting the name of the occupation into the feminine when referring to a woman, a procedure that is possible in languages that have a feminine form, such as French or Spanish. Alternatively, the noun itself can be transformed. In English, for example, one can use 'mail carrier' instead of 'postman', 'fire-fighter' instead of 'fireman', etc.

GRAMMAR AND SYNTAX

The French grammatical rule that adjectives and past participles take the masculine form when there are two or more subjects of different sexes is a sexist rule and should certainly be changed. The use of masculine plural pronouns in French and Spanish to designate persons of both the male and the female sex should also be revised.

The Kuwaiti study observes that in Arabic also the masculine form is used when there are plural subjects of different sexes. It proposed remedying this inequality by using the plural pronoun, as in the Arabic equivalent of the following English phrase: 'average Arabs drink *their* coffee black' instead of 'the average Arab drinks *his* coffee black'.

As the rules of vocabulary, grammar and syntax differ from one language to another, grammarians and linguists working in each language will have to introduce appropriate changes to eliminate all sexist connotations.

5. Action to eliminate sexism in the school system

It has already been noted that sexism, as it occurs in school textbooks and at school, is merely a reflection of the sexism that prevails in society as a whole. Consequently, in order to eliminate sexism, both from textbooks and from the world of school, action must not be confined to the school system alone.

This system involves a multitude of individuals with social roles, who may or may not have been sensitized to the existence of sexist stereotypes in school textbooks. Action should therefore be taken towards each part of the system: ministries of education and/or culture, administrative or teaching staff in schools, guidance counsellors and education advisers, and, finally, the pupils themselves. Action may be undertaken simultaneously or serially among all those concerned, depending on the situation and the resources available. I shall give several examples of action that has already been taken, as well as a number of suggestions, concentrating my attention on action aimed at ministries or departments of education and culture, administrative and non-teaching personnel in schools, teaching staff and educators, guidance counsellors and educational advisers, and pupils.

Such action may consist of awareness development, training or legislation. For reasons of clarity, I shall not attempt to classify the different types of action separately, as each is closely interrelated with the others: thus, all anti-sexist legislation relating to schools is itself a means of developing awareness, and has pedagogical value. Likewise, work of awareness development may be carried out in the context of training seminars.

Action towards ministries or departments of education and culture

Of all ministries, those most concerned are obviously the ministries of education and/or culture, since they supervise, closely or otherwise, depending on the country, the education system in force. However, if the ministry of education or the ministry of culture is responsible for planning, designing and illustrating school textbooks, the action to be taken will differ from action towards the private sector, when the latter has those responsibilities.

In the former case, action aimed at a ministry of education or of culture will depend primarily on whether or not the government wishes sexism to disappear from school textbooks. If the authorities agree about this priority, the ministries concerned will confer with the relevant social agents: publishing houses, authors, illustrators, etc.

Theoretically, it should be easier to stamp out sexism from school textbooks in countries with a planned economy, where the production of textbooks by publishing houses is very much the responsibility of the authorities, and takes place under their supervision.

In countries with a market economy, where the design and production of children's books and school textbooks are largely the responsibility of the private sector, action taken towards ministries, departments or institutes depends to a greater extent on the wishes of the general public, or on the initiatives of a ministry with special responsibility for women's rights. At the first stage, the influence that may be exerted by public opinion on the ministry or department of education is expressed through the agency of the feminist movements, which are responsible for more and more studies, articles in the press and meetings denouncing sexist stereotypes in textbooks. In the United States, for example, feminists have carried out excellent research work followed by campaigns, as in New Jersey, where they denounced the existence of sexism in American school textbooks, on the strength of an analysis of 2,760 stories published in 134 textbooks in use in the primary schools of that state in 1972 [31]. In the same year, Weitzman published an article on sex-role socialization in the *American Journal of Sociology* [32]. In 1974, feminists in the Department of Psychology of the University of Michigan (Ann Arbor) launched a periodical entitled *Sex Discrimination in Education Newsletter*, which proposed to combat sexism in the education system, particularly in school textbooks, while at the same time a basic work covering all aspects of sexism in the American education system was published as a paperback entitled *And Jill Came Tumbling After: Sexism in American Education* [17]. This campaign was enhanced by university-level publications written by women graduates, who, as early as 1970, had taught women's studies in American universities (such as Béreaud at Cornell University or Weitzman at the University of California), and it came to the attention of the authorities in the United States Department of Health, Education and Welfare (HEW).

In France, the action taken towards the education ministry by feminists at the beginning of the 1970s, regarding sexism in school textbooks, was supported by the Ministère des Droits de la Femme (Ministry for Women's Rights). At the latter's instigation, the education ministry issued a departmental order, published in the *Bulletin officiel* of 22 July 1982, which stipulated that as from the 1982/83 school year, an educational campaign against sexist prejudice should be launched 'to combat sexist prejudice in all curricula, for all school subjects and educational activities, at all levels of primary and secondary education'. Furthermore, the Ministère des Droits de la Femme has established a commission to eliminate sexism in school textbooks within the Paris education district, whose first aim will be to make an overall survey of the field. The commission's members are superintendents of schools and representatives of teachers' unions, parent associations and the Ministère des Droits de la Femme. It has become apparent that the principle of academic freedom for teachers is sometimes invoked to mask resistance to change on the part of administrative and education authorities, the education ministry and the various districts under its control.

Action aimed at the ministries may impel them to bring pressure to bear on the public servants who are answerable to them (teachers, instructors, guidance counsellors, etc.) or on the publishers and authors of textbooks and children's literature.

Action towards administrative and non-teaching personnel in schools

These types of action are extremely diverse and may be initiated by several groups: local associations, ministries, feminist groups, etc.

In France, for instance, the Association pour une Éducation Non Sexiste (Association for Non-sexist Education) has waged a dynamic campaign aimed at the head-teachers of schools. It proposes to 'combat the traditional portrayal of male and female roles as reproduced in the illustrations and the text of school textbooks; to foster awareness among teachers, parents, parent associations, head teachers, school inspectors, local councillors, publishers and authors, regarding the sexist features of school textbooks' [33].

Following the action by the Ministère des Droits de la Femme, the French education ministry issued a departmental order (July 1982) making the directors of all primary, middle and upper secondary schools and all heads of department for physical education, each in his or her own field, responsible for the implementation of the educational campaign against sexist prejudice at school.

In the United States, the Education Amendment of October 1976, issued by the HEW, stipulated that a minimum of $50,000 would be granted each year to every American state that established, in conjunction with the state education office or any other appropriate agency, a special bureau responsible for eliminating sexist stereotypes in education curricula. This legislation may be of assistance to

American schools that are planning to embark on the elimination of sexist stereotypes from curricula and school textbooks.

Since 1974, Norway has been supplying the head teachers and staff of primary schools and of lower secondary schools with a national education syllabus designed to eliminate sexism from school textbooks. Likewise, in the Federal Republic of Germany, a commission has been set up which recommended that all school equipment and textbooks be vetted in order to 'eliminate' all clichés about roles'. In Austria, an intergovernmental working group has produced a guide to the portrayal of men and women and of family life in school textbooks in a non-sexist manner. Although this guide was compiled in November 1980, 'it will take some years before significant changes will be seen' [34, p. 134].

By setting up specific commissions, either within a ministry of education or of culture, or within the regional or local governments corresponding to the location of the schools, it should be possible to sensitize school administrators to the problem of sexism.

In countries with a planned economy, there are no reports of action aimed at school administrators, as school textbooks are supplied directly to schools by the departments of culture or of education, which supervise their production in state publishing houses. Accordingly, action directed at the publishing houses and at authors of textbooks plays a predominant part in such countries, whereas in countries with a market economy action is diversified and aimed at various different targets—school administrators, teachers, parents, etc.

The Kuwaiti study [25] suggests encouraging school libraries to balance their choice of children's books: books on both women and men, books written by both women and men.

It has already been observed that sexism at school also finds expression in the hierarchy of school administration, since headships and positions of authority are usually reserved for men, whereas the posts requiring the performance of duties (essentially teaching posts) go to women. It will thus not suffice for ministries of education or head teachers to modify the content of school textbooks in order to foster the full development of children's potential, if the very structure of the school system remains sexist and constitutes a model for stereotyped roles of men and women in society. The suggestions addressed by the Commission of European Communities to ministries of education regarding changes in the structure of school systems in Member States should be recalled:

There seems a need to develop positive national policies to encourage: (a) more men teachers to teach in the primary sector; (b) more women to seek secondary headships and deputy headships or supervisory posts; (c) more women to train to teach subjects hitherto dominated by men and vice versa; (d) further inquiry into the actual work and duties assigned to women and men in secondary schools to attack sex stereotyping of roles [22, para. 2.64].

One might add to this directive the recommendation that the ministries of education of the countries of the European Community, and, indeed, of other countries, should also enable women to play a more equitable role in 'higher' education, so that trainee teachers taking university courses may be convinced that women and men are equals at whatever education level.

Action towards teaching staff and educators

Action to influence teaching staff appears, in most countries, to be one of the keys to success in eradicating sexism at school. For example, according to the Ukrainian study, 'The indispensable condition for success in this matter is educators' firm belief in the importance of eliminating negative stereotypes, their knowledge of major factors and consistent patterns of their manifestation in different age-groups . . .' [11, p. 45].

In countries where most school textbooks are written by teachers, or by supervisors still in office or in retirement, the role of teachers in the elimination of sexism emerges as decisive. However, this should not give rise to naïve optimism: teachers, after all, differ very little from other social agents (ministry officials, school administrators, parents, publishers, etc.). They have all been conditioned since childhood to take for granted the traditional division of domestic and occupational tasks according to sexist stereotypes. The fact that primary-school teachers are relatively young, and for the most part female, offers no guarantee against the existence of sexism at school and in school textbooks. It is thus essentially through voluntary action, aimed at all administrative and teaching staff in primary and secondary education, that results can be obtained. Such action may be launched by the teachers, by private concerns, or by the ministries. It may consist of different types of individual or group action, in which awareness development and training are essential, but it cannot be confined to these, and must widen its scope to include changing the sexist attitudes of teachers towards their pupils.

In France, the various drives to sensitize and train teachers in anti-sexism have been started concomitantly by private associations, the Ministère des Droits de la Femme and teachers.

For example, the Association pour une Éducation Non Sexiste has made teachers aware of the problem of sexism in school textbooks and education by organizing several kinds of activity: numerous seminars, to which not only teachers but parents, trade unionists, representatives of various associations and feminists were invited; the projection, during those seminars, of films and video cassettes (including one on sexism in school textbooks and at school, entitled *The Domestic Help and the Businessman*); distribution to teachers of McGraw-Hill's guide (intended for authors of educational materials) and of a set of analytical questions to be used to identify sexism in school textbooks; and finally, the sale or renting out of display panels on sexism at school and in textbooks that teachers can also use to instruct pupils in anti-sexism.

The Ministère des Droits de la Femme considers that anti-sexist action must include teacher training that takes respect for others as its first principle. According to the statistics, respect for others is a priority for only 29 per cent of French teachers [36, p. 13]. Furthermore, in the view of the ministry, learning to respect others cannot be an abstract process but can be attained only through the rejection of sex stereotypes.

If awareness of others is not based on an analysis of sex stereotypes, which all constitute obstacles and prisons, and which Simone de Beauvoir has called 'pretty pictures', then respect for others remains a matter of lip-service. So teacher training of the type in question can be effective by inducing student teachers to analyse stereotypes and images by means of an additional form of training [36, p. 13].

The French education ministry's departmental order of July 1982 stipulated that

educators have a fundamental part to play in action to combat sexist prejudice, each in the context of his or her own educational duties, in order to help bring about a change of attitude and the elimination of all discrimination against women. . . . Educators must identify and criticize in all teaching material (textbooks, information sheets, slides, films, cassettes, etc.) any sexist stereotypes which may remain and which perpetuate a non-egalitarian image of women. They must also take care not to put across sexist stereotypes themselves, in either speech or conduct.

We can expect these recommendations to go unheeded until anti-sexist education is conducted among teachers, with their participation. It was with such an aim in mind that a primary-school supervisor developed this form of education in a French teacher-training institution. She considered that in order to tackle the problem of sexism in school textbooks, it is obviously necessary to include the teachers; that is to say, to include them in any action and not be content with supplying them with educational materials that they may well regard as an end and not a means.

The experiment took the form of a two-week further training course organized by the teacher-training institution of the town of Nantes, for the benefit of teachers in the region. It should be noted that French teachers resist change in the name of academic freedom for teachers, as if the defence of this freedom had something to do with the defence of the right of human beings, whether men or women, to dignity. But what sense does it make to repudiate the rights of women in the name of respect for academic freedom?

In the United States, in response to pressure brought to bear by feminist organizations and researchers at universities, many types of action have been undertaken against sexism in schools, particularly where teachers are concerned. The *Born Free* programme [35] was developed in 1976 by the Counselling and Student Personnel Psychology Director of the College of Education of the University of Minnesota. This programme is aimed at a reduction in sexist stereotypes in education institutions as these affect both men and women. The main task is to produce instructive material for parents and teachers at every education level (primary, secondary and post-secondary).

The original experiment, which was intended principally for teachers and for the parents of their pupils, entailed attending a training workshop for one year. In the course of the workshop, the forty participants learnt that they could change their personal attitudes and conduct, or their interpersonal behaviour in the classroom or with colleagues, or they could help to change the organizational structures of their institution, or they could do all three at once. After this workshop, the participants were divided into fourteen educator teams and carried out sixty-four different activities aimed at reducing sexism in education. In most cases, they organized two-day training sessions known as 'staff development projects', for small groups made up of teachers, sometimes also of parents who took time off work in order to attend. At these training sessions the participants exchanged impressions of their own socialization with respect to family and occupational roles—an exercise which, according to the author of the project, might not be acceptable in all cultures. This introspection within a small group enabled the American teachers and parents involved to gain a better understanding of the influence they exert over children. As the author of the *Born Free* programme goes on to note, this training is essentially cognitive, as teachers and parents are taught to recognize the facts of distribution of the sex roles; it also has an experiential and affective side, the implication being that the educators understand the negative consequences of sexist stereotypes on children and become aware of the most subtle sexist attitudes and forms of behaviour.

To sum up, it is tempting to say that the philosophy of the *Born Free* programme is based on the Socratic precept 'know thyself'. The teacher learns to gain a better understanding of the way roles are distributed in society between men and women, how he/she acts towards pupils and how he/she can remedy sexist discrimination in the field of education.

This programme also includes a very precise strategy whose aim is to induce teachers, in the course of a 90-minute meeting, to pick out sexist stereotypes in school textbooks. A questionnaire for assessing sexism, as well as one or two textbooks, are distributed to them, and they are asked to evaluate the textbooks with the help of the special questionnaire (Table 4). Three-quarters of an hour later, the whole group discusses the results of the assessment and, if sufficient time remains, a complete list is drawn up of all the sexist stereotypes found.

These training sessions—which take place during working hours with the agreement of the school principal—require teachers to assume an active role in increasing consciousness concerning the sexist stereotypes to be found in school textbooks.

Training future teachers in teacher-training establishments to combat sexism is recommended by the Norwegian study:

For textbooks to be better it is necessary for the users—teachers and pupils—to be aware of the rules in force and the demands that should be made. . . . The team proposes that the *Guidelines on Equal Status* should be made known to teachers and pupils. . . . Students at colleges of education and teachers should be trained in the analysis of textbooks on the basis of equal status as part of their teacher training or in-service training [12, p. 91].

Bisaria [5] also suggests that this type of approach be adopted towards teachers and future teachers in India and Asia in general. Training programmes for teachers must be assertive about anti-sexism. The curricula of teacher-training institutions must be carefully examined, and any persistent sexist tendencies weeded out. Until a whole generation of students, from school to university, has freed itself from stereotypes, the utmost attention must be paid to the preparation of syllabuses and prospectuses for the training of teachers.

The Peruvian study [21] also suggests fostering awareness among teachers, in particular by means

TABLE 4. Evaluating educational materials

In order to assess the degree to which educational materials may perpetuate sex-role stereotyping, answer the following questions:

1. Title of text/material:

2. Subject matter:

3. Copyright owner (year):

4. Author(s):
   Sex of author(s): Female   Male

5. What activities/occupations are mentioned or pictured for:
   Girls   *Boys*   *Women*   *Men*

6. How many pictures of each sex are shown:
   Girls   *Boys*   *Women*   *Men*

7. How many times does the text mention:
   Women/Girls   *Men/Boys*

8. What adjectives are used to describe:
   Girls   *Boys*   *Women*   *Men*

9. Describe the language used throughout the text. Is it non-sexist and inclusive in nature?

10. Are significant contributions of women or men omitted?

11. Are traditional stereotypes upheld for the different groups, in terms of activities, interests, family roles, occupations, etc.? What kinds of role models are depicted for boys and girls?

12. Is the material portrayed in a contemporary, realistic style?

13. Are there special sections dealing solely with women and ethnic populations?

14. How might these materials have an impact on educational/occupational aspirations for girls and boys?

15. Summarize your analysis of the text/material in one page or less.

Source: Born Free programme, University of Minnesota, United States [35, p. 87–8].

of the report prepared on the subject in Peru, which should be circulated to teacher-training institutions; it adds that teachers should be required to participate in the preparation of educational materials, and recommends that men and women attend training courses together.

The Quebec study [2] provides for the circulation to representatives of the different groups concerned, including teachers, of a series of recommendations and suggestions designed to help users to be on the alert for any sexist educational materials currently in circulation, as a prelude, of course, to the production of non-sexist textbooks. It also asks

that school commissions and schools should reassess the materials that they are using at present by forming special committees, which could become permanent, and subsequently study other sex-linked discriminatory factors in the organization of schools, . . . and that teachers should look into the mechanisms whereby sexist attitudes are passed on by the school and attempt to determine their own roles in the formation or reinforcement of such attitudes among their pupils [2, p. 184].

It is evident that most authors of studies on sexism in school textbooks consider teacher training to be fundamental. More often than not, such training extends beyond school textbooks, since it also aims to make teachers more aware, whether during their initial training or during their teaching career, of their responsibilities in this area; it would naturally be futile to attempt to eliminate sexism from school textbooks if it persisted in the relations between teachers and their pupils. Consequently, with this aim in mind, the Canadian Committee on the Status of Women of the Government of Quebec proposes to issue teachers with a questionnaire intended to enable each one personally to assess his or her own behaviour towards his or her pupils of both sexes. The questionnaire is reproduced here in full because, either as it stands or with modifications, it lends itself readily to use in the training of teachers (Table 5).

The use of video in classrooms has now made it possible to record pupils' behaviour as effectively as teachers' changes in attitude towards them according to their sex [38]. Consequently, its use could further new awareness of sexism in teacher/pupil relationships in the course of the teacher-training seminars.

Action towards guidance counsellors and education advisers

Although the foregoing suggestions are intended not only for teachers but for all educators, special mention should be made of the action to be taken towards education advisers and educational and vocational guidance counsellors. The importance of such action is stressed in the study carried out in Asia and the Pacific [5]: in school guidance and counselling programmes, the strategy should help to break down the social restrictions that have been imposed by the segregation of the sexes. In India, research programmes have been devised to this end for use by education advisers.

In France, it is acknowledged that sexist stereotypes influence the choices made by girls, over 80 per cent of whom usually aim for a traditional profession. Training received by girls covers some thirty specialized fields, against three hundred for boys! Such a situation arises, to a large extent at least, from the fact that girls are not sufficiently well-informed; nor are the advisers and counsellors, who too often steer them towards traditional occupations.

In the United States, feminists and those who are anxious to develop the potential abilities of all children, without exception, are very much aware that sexist stereotypes are kept alive among children of both sexes by education advisers. The main criticism to be levelled at these advisers is their ignorance of egalitarian legislation (and the harmful effects of that ignorance); their choosing to steer children, and more particularly girls, exclusively towards traditional occupations; the use they make of tests, manuals and 'career guides' larded with sexist stereotypes; their way of saying 'he' when discussing traditional male activities and 'she' for those that are allegedly for females; and the linguistic use they make of masculine terms to designate certain occupations, for instance 'fireman' instead of 'firefighter', or 'postman' instead of 'mail carrier'. They

TABLE 5. Questionnaire

Teachers, are you guilty of sexist discrimination in your class?[1]

1. Do you generally ask the boys in your class to carry out the heavier work (for instance, carrying a box) and the girls to do the lighter work (for instance, watering the plants)?
2. In group work, do you suggest to the girls that they perform secretarial duties and to the boys that they organize and give orders?
3. Have you a tendency to segregate girls from boys, either by asking them to hand in their homework separately, or by assigning them distinct roles in the performance of work, or simply by making them sit on 'their' side of the classroom?
4. Do you feel sorry for girls who are unable or unwilling to look elegant? Do you on occasion draw attention to those who look most fashionable or have the best hairstyles?
5. Do you feel sorry for boys who are clumsy or who take little interest in sport? Do you sometimes draw attention to those who are more athletic than the rest?
6. Do you react negatively to boys with long hair or those who wear medallions or bracelets, or to girls who wear trousers?
7. Do you expect boys to speak louder and less grammatically than girls?
8. Do you expect girls to express themselves better than boys?
9. Do you consider that science and mathematics coincide better with boys' interests, and reading with those of girls?
10. Do you consider it more usual to see a boy jostle a girl than the opposite?
11. Do you refrain from intervening when the boys make fun of the girls, and say to yourself that it is a sign of virility?
12. Have you ever made a boy sit next to a girl as a punishment?
13. In your school, do boys and girls have separate sections in the playground, cloakrooms or library?
14. Are the pupils made to choose practical activities according to their sex: cooking and sewing for girls, carpentry and mechanics for boys?
15. Does your school encourage girls as much as it does boys to engage in sporting activities (choice of sport, hours of access to equipment, instructors, budget, prominence given to competitive events)?
16. Do you find the following traits more or less agreeable in one or the other sex?

independent attitude	dependent nature
self-assurance, thoughtfulness	untidy work
self-assurance, self-confidence	the habit of swearing
sensitive, dreamy nature	shyness, lack of initiative
docility	qualities of leadership
sloppy appearance or bad posture	ambition, competitiveness

17. Do you think it more important to prepare boys for a successful career rather than for a successful family life?
18. Do you apply double standards for boys and girls?

1. Source: *L'école sexiste, c'est quoi?* [37].

are also criticized for their unconscious, non-verbal behaviour, which fosters the idea among pupils that there are appropriate or inappropriate options for each sex, and thus discourages or, at the very least, ignores any non-traditional choice of subject or occupation that may be formulated by certain pupils, instead of giving encouragement [35].

In order to reduce and eliminate sexism on the part of advisory boards, the University of Minnesota's *Born Free* programme proposes not only to eliminate all manifestations of sexism in tests and questionnaires for students, and from educational materials as a whole, but also to invite education counsellors and advisers to seminars that would count as part of their working day. At these seminars, which would last several days, the counsellors and advisers would participate on an equal footing with teachers and parents in developing their sensitivity to stereotyped attitudes and behaviour linked to the sex of their pupils, both as a group and on an individual basis, and to the sexist stereotypes embedded in the school system, educational materials, tests, textbooks, etc. Furthermore, starting from the realization that the sciences and mathematics are taught in such a way as to give boys strong motivation and to discourage girls from taking an interest in these disciplines, many countries, in particular the United States, the United Kingdom, Sweden and Norway, have adopted special programmes to change this situation and give incentives to girls [35].

All the studies make provision for the training of teachers and of all educators in anti-sexism, from the teacher-training institution onwards, or plan to organize in-service training; but it is still necessary to reach agreement on the guiding principles that should underlie this training. The Commission of European Communities lays down several guidelines that should govern anti-sexist education, in both teacher-training institutions and in-service courses:

There is a need to introduce material on sex roles in education, on the effect of organization on girls and boys, and on women's status in society, to all programmes of initial teacher training. There is little information available about the content of current courses but informed opinion suggests that very few teacher-training institutions include 'women's studies' or the implications of sex differences in schools in their basic programmes. The added problem of teachers' underexposure to the external world of work leaves them ill-equipped to counteract girls' (or boys') traditional attitudes. In particular we need to inject into all teacher-training programmes the newer approaches to counteract the effects of early childhood preconditioning to set patterns of behaviour. The concepts of any overall or homogeneous 'masculinity' and 'femininity' need especially to be questioned in educative terms. There are more differences within than between sexes [22, Para. 2.66].

In other words, training teachers to reject sexism in school textbooks implies training them to repudiate sexism, an affront to the dignity of women, in all its forms.

Action towards pupils

The majority of the studies prepared at Unesco's request recommend that teachers endeavour in their classes to awaken the pupils' critical faculties, in particular with respect to the content of school textbooks, so that they come to reject sexism. The importance of this role assigned to teachers is stressed in the Norwegian study in the following terms:

It is important that teachers, through their attitudes and textbooks, through their presentation and selection of material, should give a well-nuanced picture of reality and by means of factual information counteract discriminatory attitudes. Pupils should be prepared for life in the family, at work and in society in such a way that they are made to understand that it is natural for people, irrespective of sex, to share work and responsibility in all areas of society [12, p. 97].

The Canadian study also recommends that 'teachers should encourage among their pupils (in discussions and in everyday exercises . . .) a critical attitude towards the stereotyped images of the two sexes proffered by the educational materials available to them' [2, p. 184].

According to the University of Minnesota's *Born Free* programme, action to be undertaken with pupils must include the following steps [35]:

Ensuring that pupils are familiar with legislation on the equal status of the sexes, and related rights, including the procedure for lodging complaints in cases of discrimination.

Helping them to recognize the many forms that can be taken by sexist stereotypes in school, and their negative effects; helping them to understand their own socialization.

Teaching them to think about the education they receive and to examine it in a critical manner, and to discern sexist stereotypes and prejudice in school textbooks, curricula and educational and vocational guidance, as well as in the attitudes of the teaching staff towards them.

Teaching them that they can be agents of change in this field by working to create a juster society, and helping them to prepare for this.

Making them aware that it is important for boys and girls to be physically fit, and thus encouraging each individual, of whatever sex, to engage in a sporting activity; stressing the idea that there should be equal participation and equal opportunities for all.

Making girls understand that no subjects are exclusively reserved for one sex or the other, and that girls, just like boys, can study mathematics or any other scientific discipline, or learn a trade that is supposedly male-oriented. To boys, in their turn, it will be made clear that, just like girls, they can do housework, take care of children, or engage in any other activity that has been considered hitherto to be suitable for girls only.

The aim of the *Born Free* programme is thus to give all pupils a non-sexist education in all fields. Such a programme is obviously inconceivable without the assistance of teachers. For their benefit, and particularly for that of primary-school teachers, a guide entitled *Equal Their Chances* [39] has been written, to enable teachers to help children to identify the different manifestations of sexism. Nevertheless, it is not enough to reject negative images: there must be creative innovations that show girls and women in a more positive light, and girls must be given more precise and up-to-date information regarding the various possibilities open to them, particularly in the fields of education and occupation, in such a way as to help them come to terms with themselves as females. Such an approach will enable them to enlarge their perception of the possibilities open to them in education, employment and family life; it will help them to realize that they can control their lives; it will perhaps offer them the opportunity and the experience of occupying a management position at work, and so on.

In the *Born Free* experiment, everything seems to indicate that children's awareness of sexism in school textbooks is indissociable from educational efforts by teachers or any other educators. These efforts must not only imply the rejection of negative stereotypes, but must also be coupled with the assertion of positive images of the female sex, in such a way as to instil in girls a sense of their dignity and their equality with boys.

In France, although a ministerial order has asked teachers to pick out and criticize all forms of sexism in school textbooks, it is still necessary, once they have been sensitized to this problem and are capable of identifying the content of a textbook as sexist, that they know how to proceed with respect to their pupils. It is to the credit of the Association pour Une Éducation Non Sexiste that it supplies educational materials to teachers who wish to take action. These materials consist mainly of an 'exhibition kit' containing twenty-six double-sided panels, which are a miniature version of the panels of a large exhibition covering 100 square metres, intended for the general public. It also contains games, slides and video cassettes, to be used by the teacher with the pupils and intended to spark off a class discussion on sexism. If they wish to go more deeply into the subject with their pupils, teachers may ask a member of the association for assistance.

The Peruvian study [21] suggests using television to put across to children images that are less sexist and closer to reality.

This chapter concludes with the observation that all the studies mentioned show that sexism permeates the entire education system, occurring both in school textbooks and children's literature, and in the behaviour of the various categories of education staff. Consequently, in order to eliminate sexism, it is not enough merely to confine action to revising children's literature and textbooks. The *Born Free* programme [35] also acknowledges this fact: purging school textbooks of sexist stereotypes is necessary, but will not suffice to solve the problem of sexism at school if no changes are made in other educational materials as well, if teachers do not become aware that their behaviour towards boys and girls is biased or preferential, if there are not more women in administrative and management positions, and if changes are not made, too, to the structures of schools, which give different opportunities and hopes to boys and to girls. Such changes are also necessary in universities and in teacher-training institutions.

The need to influence a variety of people in positions of responsibility in education in order to eradicate sexism from schools makes it difficult to establish an order of priority for the action to be taken. Admittedly, it will always be easier for a country with a planned economy to take direct action to prohibit sexism in school textbooks or children's literature, but such a move will not provide a complete solution to the problem of sexism in schools, because it may still prevail in teachers' attitudes towards their pupils, or in the hierarchy of the education system, which has sexism built into it. Consequently, it seems desirable to regard anti-sexist action within the school system as being the co-ordinated co-existence of a multitude of ventures directed at all the agents involved, in all aspects of education.

Bearing these points in mind, the Council of Europe [40, pp. 3–4] has adopted a Resolution (following the Hønefoss symposium in Norway) which can be used as a basis for future programmes to eliminate sexism at school. It requires the co-ordination of various types of action, which should aim at: collecting statistics that clearly bring out the differences in the way boys and girls are treated in the school system; training teachers and all school staff, with the help of video, to become aware of their own behaviour towards pupils and supplying them, from the teacher-training institutions onwards, with a grounding in the sex-linked distinctions still observed in schools; recruiting more women for scientific and technical teaching posts and for decision-making positions within the school system; eliminating sexism from all educational materials and curricula; and offering girls the broadest possible spectrum of schooling and of career prospects, so that they can make an informed choice of the studies or occupations that they will subsequently take up.

6. Action to eliminate sexism outside the school system

Action outside the school system should deal first and foremost with the producers of school textbooks and children's literature (publishers, authors and illustrators), consumers (local authorities and parents), the mass media that broadcast information to the general public, associations, and, finally, employers who are in a position to recruit staff.

Action towards publishers, authors and illustrators of school textbooks and children's literature

Action to be directed at publishers, authors and illustrators of school textbooks and children's literature will be determined by the cultural production system of which these people are a part. In countries with a planned economy, where children's books and school textbooks are produced under the supervision of a ministry of education or of culture, initiatives in this field come from above, whereas they stem from the grass-roots in countries with a market economy, where the commercial law of profit usually determines the choices made by publishing houses in the private sector concerning books to be published for children. In both systems, specific problems arise.

In China, for example, the compilation and publication of school textbooks for primary and lower secondary education have for the most part been handled by the People's Educational Publishing House, attached to the Ministry of Education and placed under the authority of the Council for Affairs of State. Children's literature is produced mainly by the major specialized publishing houses in Beijing and Shanghai, under the control of the Ministry of Culture. Consequently, it is easy for the education and culture ministries to plan a whole series of priority moves aimed at publishing houses and authors. For example, the Ministry of Education proposes to take action on two fronts—prevention of sexism and teacher training (these two forms of action being related). Where prevention is concerned, for instance, the ministry asks those responsible for examining and approving the content of children's literature and school textbooks to be stricter: '[The latter] should fully revise any works which are inconsistent with the spirit of equality between men and women after consulting with the author and eliminate any problems which may arise before these works reach the little readers' [10, p. 67].

With regard to awareness development and training, the Ministry of Culture plans to publicize both the general blueprint for research work, as proposed by Unesco for the participants in the series of national studies on sexist prejudice, and the corresponding study undertaken in China. These will be circulated, in the first place, to all major children's publishing houses in China as well as to editorial boards or departments with a certain amount of influence and, in the second place, to authors and educators, so that they may all 'understand and pay adequate attention to the contents of the report and the problem under study' [10, p. 67].

Furthermore, it is planned to organize 'an appropriate explanation campaign' on a national scale with a view to sensitizing the country to the problem of inequality in children's literature and school textbooks. This campaign will be launched at a plenary session of the National Children's Culture and Art Committee, attended by the directors of cultural bureaux of all provinces, officials from the central government departments concerned, and authors and illustrators from various parts of China. These will be the agents of change at the local level. Plans are also being made to organize training seminars throughout the country for writers of children's books and then to make use of national organizations (the Chinese Women's Federation, the National Children's Co-ordinating Committee), etc.

The Ministry of Culture is planning a campaign using incentives based on equal representation of men and women in the text and illustrations of children's literature, because it is necessary to 'give timely encouragement to fine works and pertinent comments on the defective works' [10, p. 67].

Action in China is thus aimed at introducing better preventive measures, combined with vertical awareness development/training, starting from the top (the culture or education ministries) and extending to the authors and illustrators of children's literature and school textbooks throughout the country.

The Ukrainian Research Institute of Pedagogics also considers it of fundamental importance that the education authorities take action to influence authors and producers of children's books. The Ukrainian study suggests

The creation by the Ukrainian SSR Ministry of Education, the Research Institute of Philosophy under the Ukrainian SSR Academy of Sciences, the Research Institute of Pedagogics, the Research Institute of Psychology, teacher-training colleges and universities of the Ukraine of a task force which will elaborate recommendations for further elimination of false images (not only those which include demographic, ethnic, aesthetic and other aspects) [11, p. 43].

These recommendations, which will be finalized on the basis of the study carried out in the Ukraine within the framework of Unesco's series of national studies, are to be circulated to authors of literary works and school textbooks and to editors of periodicals and children's book series.

In Peru, although the design and production of school textbooks are the responsibility of private firms, an official assessment system has been instituted for school textbooks, which must meet certain conditions in order to be used in education establishments, as the Ministry of Education considers it necessary to 'ensure that school textbooks give genuine guidance to students in their learning' (Ministerial Decisions 2114–69 and 2115–69). 'In order to do so, commissions were set up and the minimum conditions that must be met by school textbooks were laid down' [41, pp. 21–2]. However, as the Instituto Nacional de Investigación y Desarrollo de la Educación (National Institute for Educational Research and Development), a body that is part of the Peruvian state education system, has so far disregarded the question of sexist stereotypes when granting or refusing its approval of the sale of a school textbook and its use in schools, it is urgent that this criterion be adopted as one of the essential conditions that must be met. In addition, the authors of the Peruvian study [21] recommend that the institute approach authors and publishers of school textbooks in order to make them more aware of the problem of sexist stereotypes in textbooks and oblige them to compile new textbooks that are non-sexist. A two-pronged campaign of monitoring and prevention is thus being planned to combat sexism in schools.

The author of the Zambian study considers that the authorities should take into account a major problem linked to the use of English as a lingua franca by various ethnic groups, since the English textbooks used in schools are generally written by foreign authors who, not being part of Zambian culture, 'can only imagine and superficially portray what it is to be a Zambian. It is very possible for him or her to exaggerate in one way or another the representation of the sexes in the textbooks and children's literature' [20, p. 24]. It is thus important, in order to rectify this handicap,

that the local people—in this case the Zambians—be the writers of textbooks and literature used by the children. It is the Zambians who know and have a deep feeling for the culture of its peoples. It is the Zambians who on objective reflection know what sexist biases Zambians hold and how these can be rectified [20, pp. 23–4].

The author goes on to recommend strongly that as far as possible there should be joint authorships of textbooks by Zambian men and women in order to portray youth and adults of both sexes correctly and equally. This will of course demand that the authors concerned believe deeply in the importance of equality between men and women. . . . In most cases as things stand now in Zambia there will be less women writers than male writers. Even in such cases, female participation in the production of books must be sought: women, we recommend, should sit on the curriculum and subject committees of the examination council [the body responsible for curriculum development] of the Republic of Zambia [20, p. 24].

The need to increase women's participation in the production of school textbooks is also stressed by the authors of the Norwegian study—'Publishers should make greater use of female writers and illustrators' [12, p. 90]; and by those of the Kuwaiti study [25].

In industrialized countries with a market economy, action directed at publishers and authors of children's books and school textbooks has arisen initially from feminist movements or organizations, dedicated to the cause of women's advancement and their equal status with men.

In the United States, action aimed at publishers and authors has run parallel with action aimed at the bodies responsible for education in federal or state government. The feminist groups inside or outside the universities, sometimes helped by pupils' parents, have taken action to denounce the perpetuation of stereotyped images of men and women in school textbooks, and to propose other alternatives. This action has paid off. As long ago as 1972, the publisher McGraw-Hill issued its guidelines for equal treatment of the sexes in school textbooks. McGraw-Hill's course of action has been widely adopted by other American publishers of school textbooks, who have issued authors with guides to non-sexist writing. Furthermore, following McGraw-Hill's example, publishers have appointed a larger number of feminists to their staff, members of the National Organization of Women (NOW), for instance, who are highly motivated towards helping their publishing houses to produce non-sexist textbooks. Action towards publishers has been largely a matter of convincing them that, if they continue with sexist stereotypes, their profits will suffer.

In France, the Ministry of Education has adopted the principle that school textbooks for all classes at primary and lower secondary levels are to be provided free of charge. However, while the municipalities have an annual budget for the purchase of school textbooks, it is the education minister who purchases textbooks for secondary schools. One might suppose that the ministry, being the body which pays for the textbooks used in secondary schools, would be able to bring pressure to bear on the publishers, who are its suppliers. But in fact, on grounds of authors' creative freedom, it is the publishers who decide on the content of textbooks [42].

The Association pour une Éducation Non Sexiste took the lead in approaching French publishers and asking for the eradication of all forms of sexism from school textbooks and children's literature. The association's first initiative was to send a French translation of McGraw-Hill's guidelines for equal treatment of the sexes to all French publishers of children's books and school textbooks. Drawing inspiration from this guide, some publishers of children's literature and school textbooks, such as Nathan and Magnard, made a number of anti-sexist recommendations to their authors.

Despite this venture, it seems that French publishers of school textbooks are in no hurry to have published books rewritten from an anti-sexist standpoint. The more often the same textbooks are reprinted, the lower will be production costs and the higher the profits for the publishers. The French socialist members of parliament were well aware of this when they presented a private member's bill to combat racist and sexist discrimination in school textbooks on 30 June 1980. The preamble states:

There exists a form of a discrimination which, far from being opposed or even merely avoided by the authors of textbooks, is a feature of nearly all of them: discrimination on grounds of sex. . . . One reason for this state of affairs may be the laziness of certain publishers, who reissue books unchanged that were first published thirty years ago, thereby making a substantial profit. Undoubtedly, at the time when such books first appeared, the dominant ideology imposed an extremely disparaging portrayal of girls and women, without any real objections being made. Today, women are becoming forceful in their rejection of these pejorative images; yet this is not taken into consideration: books full of clichés are reissued, and even in new books the same old errors are made. This abuse starts in the very first years of schooling.

The Socialist Party's bill was preceded on 1 March 1979 by a proposition submitted to the Senate by members of the French Communist Party requesting that 'a commission attached to the Ministry of Education be established, some members of which should be publishers' representatives, for the purpose of laying down recommendations in order to bring the portrayal of women in primary-school textbooks into line with the ideal of equality between men and women'.

In Norway, action towards publishers is today the responsibility of the Ministry of Church and Education, although Norwegian feminists such as Skjønsberg were the first to approach this ministry and urge it to turn its attention to the elimination of sexism in teaching, children's literature and school textbooks [43]. Following these efforts, an approval system was set up within the ministry to examine textbooks from the standpoint of the equality of the sexes; this body must officially approve textbooks for use in schools. If the criterion of equal status is not respected, it may ask the publisher to make changes. However, the authors of the Norwegian study suggest a number of measures that would make this approval system function more efficiently:

Closer co-operation in well-defined terms between the equal status examiners themselves, and between the equal status examiners and the Council for Primary and Lower Secondary Education and the Council for Upper Secondary Education. . . . There should be regular discussions on matters of principle in the application of the rules for approving textbooks between the equal status examiners, specialists in the various subjects, publishers and representatives of the women's organizations. . . . Publishers should be helped to understand that account must be taken of the equal status requirement from the moment that material is being selected and the book is being designed. . . . The actual enforcement of the rules for approval in respect of equality between the sexes should be made stricter [12, p. 90].

The authors also stress that 'the approval system [is] a useful tool to bring about change in textbooks and recommends that approval on the basis of equal status criteria should continue' [12, p. 89].

The Norwegian Ministry of Church and Education considers that prior approval is compatible with the untrammelled creativity of authors and with the academic freedom of teachers.

The importance of research work

Action to influence publishers and authors of school textbooks would be doomed to failure in certain disciplines, such as history, if research on the role of women in history, past and present, did not provide them with the necessary information for the writing of non-sexist textbooks. For this reason, the authors of the Norwegian study recommend, among other things, the development of research on women artists, on the conditions in which women have lived and on the contributions they have made through the ages to literature, music, art, philosophy, ideas, sociology, government, social anthropology, law and economics. Consequently, it is not enough to influence the publishers and authors of school textbooks and children's books; it is necessary at the same time to give feminists the resources they need to conduct research on women in universities and major research organizations.

The authors of the Ukrainian study [11] call for research work to be launched with a view to determining the causes of the survival of stereotyped models, which are now anachronistic, and research on the conditions that must be fulfilled in order to neutralize their influence on the formation of the child's personality.

Finally, the Council of Europe [40] recommends that research begin without delay into how changes in attitudes, behaviour and social structures come about.

Much emphasis is placed on the importance of conducting research, not only on the past and present history of women, but also on the process of resistance to social change or, alternatively, the factors that make it easier.

Action towards local authorities and parents

Most authors of the studies examined have stressed the need to enlist the participation of parents and the relevant local authorities in combating sexism at school.

Dunnigan, for example, recommends that 'parents and children should examine together the content of the latter's school textbooks, readers and favourite programmes, and discuss any stereotypes that they find in them; they should join forces in order to make known their objections, if any, to heads of schools, publishers and the media' [2, p. 184].

Abu Nasr et al. consider that it is necessary to sensitize educators, parents, students, administrators, publishers, authors, illustrators and the general public to the problem of sexism in school textbooks by:

Forming committees including people who are aware of sexist issues to help in the selection of textbooks.... Conducting seminars on textbooks and educational materials for teachers, parents, writers, publishers, illustrators and others, where sexist issues are discussed.... Disseminating evaluation results to those who produce and those who use textbooks.... Developing guidelines that may help teachers and parents to reduce the impact of biased materials on children [1, pp. 57–8].

The authors of the Peruvian study [21] think it advisable to sensitize parents to sexism in school textbooks by organizing meetings for their benefit.

The necessary action, as the French and American experiments show, may be launched either by official bodies or by private initiatives. In France, local authorities have responsibilities in the field of education, as each year they have to allocate part of the communal budget for the purchase of school textbooks for primary schools. These municipalities could, consequently, monitor the content of the textbooks. Of course, granted that it is feasible for local authorities to participate in eliminating sexism from school textbooks, it is still necessary to sensitize them to the problem. To this end, the Association pour une Éducation Non Sexiste has organized, at the local level, seminars, meetings and exhibitions, bringing together members of the municipal council responsible for education problems in their area, feminists, and representatives of parents, unions and teachers. The Ministère des Droits de la Femme has supported the association's action by setting up local commissions for combating sexism in school textbooks. These commissions may be either departmental or municipal, and their function is to read school textbooks and suggest non-sexist books for purchase by local councils which have budgets for the purpose. Furthermore, the ministry has signed several 'anti-sexist contracts' with French towns, providing for a municipal commission that will examine the content of school textbooks for examples of sexism and rectify these [44].

Action directed at parents is also one of the aims that the Association pour une Éducation Non Sexiste has set itself. Although French parents do not buy their children's school textbooks, which are supplied free of charge, they nevertheless have certain powers of decision in schools, by virtue of parents' associations. Parents' right to examine the content of school textbooks was the objective sought by the Socialist Party bill submitted in June 1980 which proposed in Article 1 that:

At the initiative of its head or one of its members, the parents' association may be required to give its opinion regarding the textbooks used in schools; it may in particular advise against their use if they appear to be discriminatory with respect to groups defined by race, sex, or political, social or religious views. Two weeks before this discussion, the textbooks in question must be made available by the head teacher to parents and teachers who wish to see them, for purposes of consultation. A joint meeting may be organized at the request of any of those concerned.

Although this bill did not become law, the Ministry of Education sent a circular recommending school principals to make a special point of keeping parents informed on matters of equal status.

The *Born Free* programme at the University of Minnesota [35] selects both teachers and parents as target groups for awareness development and training with a view to combating the main sexist stereotypes in schools and school textbooks. Thus, parents are asked to attend the same training sessions as their children's teachers (see page 68).

This programme takes as its starting-point parents' usual attitudes towards their children's education: they fail to tell them about laws of equality, and hence about children's rights; they place too much confidence in the school, instead of questioning their own practices; and they have a habit of approaching teachers individually, instead of uniting with other parents as members of parent-teacher associations working in the framework of new structures. Consequently, the aim of the sessions to which parents are invited must be to help them to acquire knowledge and understanding of sexism in schools and in society; to become competent to work towards change; to become alert to the messages conveyed to their children at school in textbooks, in their relations with teachers, in the information they are given on careers, and in school rules; to become aware that the division of labour at home may perpetuate stereotypes; to develop new systems of role-swapping in household duties; and to insist that schools use only non-sexist textbooks and educational materials.

The *Born Free* programme is based on the hypothesis that work of awareness development and training for parents with a view to the identification and rejection of sexism in school textbooks is indissociable from work to develop parents' awareness of their own sexist behaviour towards their children. The same efforts are demanded of teachers. The basic postulate of this method is that the elimination of sexism in school textbooks will do nothing to emancipate children of both sexes or to enable them to develop their full potential (by choosing varied and non-stereotyped roles), while the first individuals with whom children come into contact, i.e. parents and teachers, bind them by their habits and attitudes in the shackles of traditional sex-determined roles.

Action towards the media, the general public and associations

Action to eradicate sexism from school textbooks must be accompanied by action directed at the media.[1] The importance of such action in the developing countries is stressed by many authors.

Bisaria [5], for example, considers that the media have a decisive role to play in the education of the illiterate and the newly literate. If the audio-visual media convey sexist messages, achievements in changes to school textbooks and curricula will quickly turn out to be useless. Accordingly, all action to eliminate sexism from school curricula and textbooks, as well as in children's literature and the media, should be synchronized. Non-sexist media could constitute an education subsystem that would enrich teaching by contributing slides, educational films, cassettes, etc.

Likewise, in Spain, according to a statement made by the education ministry's representative at the Hønefoss symposium on sexism at school,

Neither school nor teachers nor pupils are an island within society, and society is full of stereotypes. This is reflected in television, advertising and the other media, which still make a traditional distinction between the roles of men and women. In all media representations, the man tends to be cast in active roles of leadership and responsibility, the woman in passive, secondary and submissive roles. . . . the woman is a consumer, shallow and superficial, defenceless or dependent—a sexual object [45, p. 190].

The need to influence the media and the general public as well as families and teachers is also stressed in the Ukrainian study:

The study team of the Ukrainian SSR also considers it feasible to arrange a socio-educational formative experiment on the problem reviewed (among different age-groups), which would make it possible to elaborate recommendations—for schools, families, mass media and public at large—on combating negative stereotypes [11, p. 46].

The Chinese study suggests mobilizing women's federations and the committees in defence of children

so that each of them plays its role in its field of work, creates public opinion and thinks up ways and means to promote from different angles equality between men and women of the whole society and regard this action as a matter of importance to beautifying the environ-

---

1. Included under this term are the images conveyed by radio, television, newspapers and magazines, strip cartoons, cassettes, etc.

ment, facilitating the sound development of the next generation and bringing direct benefit to the 300 million children and the society as a whole [10, p. 68].

The Peruvian study [21] also stresses the need to deal with sexual discrimination in the media in general, and to give publicity to research on the subject and at the same time to possible solutions. Finally, the American *Born Free* programme [35] acknowledges that, whereas in the 1970s, action against sexism at school and in school textbooks tended to focus on teachers and parents, the battle against sexism has now expanded to include the general public, thanks in particular to the action of federal agencies and community organizations. This is a development common to the United States and European societies. The Women's Bureau of the United States Department of Labor, the American Association of University Women, the Girls' League, and the Girl Scouts League, as well as other organizations, have waged national campaigns to inform the public of the restrictions placed on women's advancement as a result of inequalities based on sexual discrimination. Agencies have developed new policies with change in mind, such as programmes of positive action (in Norway, the United States and Canada), action based on equality of opportunity, etc. Meetings have taken place in the context of associations, such as women's centres, special sections of teachers' unions and religious organizations working for equality between men and women in the Church, which have made it possible to launch campaigns to reduce sexism and sexist stereotypes on television as well as in school textbooks, book illustrations, toys and the media.

In France, women journalists have drawn the attention of the public to sexism in school textbooks. The Association pour une Éducation Non Sexiste recognizes that it is very important to arouse the interest of the press, this being one of the best means of reaching teachers and providing them with information on the problem of sexism in textbooks. Other French associations, such as the Ligue des Droits de l'Homme (Human Rights League), the Union des Femmes Françaises (Union of French Women), parents' federations, teachers' or workers' unions, and women's or family organizations, have tried to sensitize their members to the problem of sexism.

Action towards employers

It may seem strange to recommend action aimed at employers in connection with the battle against sexism in school textbooks and children's literature. However, if girls are not steered more often towards non-traditional careers, and if guidance counsellors and parents do not encourage any other choice, one reason is that employers are unwilling to take on women in non-traditional occupations; they act in accordance with the sexist stereotypes that they have absorbed, like all other members of society. As long as employers have a sexist attitude, the image of stereotype occupations for men and for women will continue to prevail among individuals of both sexes, whether teachers, educators, parents, pupils, town councillors, members of an organization, publishers, writers or potential workers. The absence of women in all occupations set aside for men, and of men in so-called women's jobs, will strengthen sexist stereotypes in everyone's minds, including the authors and publishers of school textbooks and children's literature. So the barriers that employers erect to the interchangeability of occupations between the sexes have a feedback effect, and consequently reinforce sexist stereotypes. It is therefore important to educate employers too, the aim of the action being, *inter alia*, to enable every individual, of whatever sex, to develop his or her abilities and potential for work.

Sweden is usually cited as an example for having carried out programmes of positive action to break down this rigid classification of male and female jobs. The Committee for Recommendations on Equality between Women and Men, answerable to the prime minister, has proposed three reforms which have been adopted by the government:

1. The assignment of one hundred officials to local offices of the public employment service, where they would specialize in the problems of job-seeking women.

2. Employers who hire and train women or men for jobs dominated by the opposite sex would qualify for training allowances, collectively known as the 'equality subsidy'.

3. Companies would have to hire both men and women in order to qualify for state-granted regional

development aid (towards plant location, etc.). At least 40 per cent of the new jobs provided by a company must be reserved for each sex [46, p. 21].

In France, the Secrétaire d'État au Travail Féminin (Secretary of State for Women's Employment) at first established several pilot training centres [47] for women only, which trained them in so-called non-female trades, such as metal-working and welding, and they received a minimum wage during the months of training. Subsequently, the Ministère des Droits de la Femme increased to one hundred the number of courses to train women for many non-traditional occupations (horticulture, computer science, office automation, welding, car mechanics, electrical trades, etc.). Women taking these courses, which last between 9 and 12 months, are paid a minimum wage, and all the women who have sought employment in their new specialized field have found it.

Programmes of positive action with financial incentives, as outlined above, show that it is possible to break down the traditional habits of thought that link a particular trade, and the training it entails, with one sex only.

Assessment of the impact of action against sexism in children's literature and school textbooks

The foregoing shows the extent to which various countries, having studied this problem, are conscious of the need to foster awareness and provide education in anti-sexism to a large number of social agents outside the restricted circles of the teaching profession and authors and publishers of children's literature and school textbooks. However, although the intentions are explicit, few reports contain specific details about the results of the action undertaken.

In countries with a planned economy, it is an acknowledged fact that the ideals of equal status which have been written into the constitution have led to an improvement of women's status in the texts and illustrations of both children's literature and school textbooks.

In countries with a market economy, positive results have been observed as a result of action taken. In the United States, for example, several investigations indicate favourable results obtained thanks to the action of parents and educators, who successfully convinced publishers that they should eliminate sexism from school textbooks. Publishers such as McGraw-Hill and national organizations such as the National Council of Teachers of English have worked out their own code for the equal treatment of the two sexes. The changes indicated in Kepner and Koehn's study [48] include a better balance between numbers of women and men in stories, and between the numbers of heroes and heroines. Furthermore, mothers are depicted in more active roles, and some fathers work in the kitchen. By and large, sexist language has been eliminated and replaced by less sexist and more inclusive language. The examples used in science and mathematics textbooks have been revised in order to capture the interest of girls and women. Likewise, the implementation of the *Born Free* programme [35] by the bodies concerned has been followed by positive results: subsequent investigations clearly show that training material designed to combat sexism has helped the educators concerned to increase the effectiveness of their action on behalf of equal status. With even greater precision, repeated assessments of the impact of the training sessions on educators and parents show that changes take place immediately or a year later.

However, resistance on the part of the more conservative elements of American society is also stressed:

This process of eliminating sexism from textbooks, which began in the early 1970s, has been slow, primarily because new guidelines for preparing non-sexist textbooks had to be prepared and implemented, but also because a polarization process was set in motion through which conservative men and women, threatened by the proposed changes, began to protest about the imposed, undesirable new and confusing sex role messages [30, p. 119].

Other assessments carried out in the United States have shown how the effect of non-sexist images and texts on children's attitudes and behaviour can be strengthened, or otherwise, depending on individual circumstances. According to Safilios-Rothschild [30, pp. 121–2], even when the attitude of the parents does not support anti-sexist action attempted at school for children's benefit, the fact of presenting them with non-sexist texts or images produces some immediate effects. But, although children may be exposed to non-sexist models at school, the latter cannot be reinforced, as there are no schools in which all textbooks are free of sexist stereotypes. Furthermore, the anti-sexist aspect of many textbooks goes no further than balancing the number of male and female characters.

These findings can be rounded off by some remarks in the Hansen and Schultz guide [35] that may be summarized as follows: children in nursery school may be taught to take up non-sexist occupations; attitudes regarding the roles of the sexes are difficult to change in children of all ages; children are not sexist towards themselves; they tend to be sexist towards their peers of the same sex; they are much more so towards their peers of the opposite sex; girls attempt to create lifestyles in which they can combine a home and a career; boys have a tendency to scorn or repress non-sexist values; the role allotted to boys is perceived by children as being more rigid than that devolving on girls and women, which they see as more flexible; and to give children the slightest sign of favouring sexism is or may be dangerous, whereas the adoption of a firm and assured position may have an extremely beneficial effect. Finally, among other strategies, traditional male stereotypes in school textbooks should be changed more often, since they lead boys to believe that they are the superior sex.

The authors of the Norwegian study [12] consider that the approval system used by the Ministry of Church and Education for school textbooks and children's literature should be made more efficient, in view of the fact that there are still far too many sexist texts and illustrations in these books.

In France, the Association pour une Éducation Non Sexiste feels that few results have been obtained where school textbooks are concerned. Some people ascribe this sluggishness to the meagre sums of money allocated by the local authorities for the purchase of primary-school textbooks. However, the Délégation Régionale à la Condition Féminine (Regional Delegation on the Status of Women) of the Ile de France region has won some measure of success [49].

A list of the various attempts to date to eliminate sexism among publishers and writers of children's literature and textbooks, parents, municipalities, the media, the general public, organizations and employers, shows that highly diverse strategies have been used to attain the stated aim. Training activities, courses, seminars, symposia, articles by journalists on the radio and in the press, and television programmes can trigger off group action outside the school system, the first stage being awareness development among the general public. However, it is still necessary for the initiators of such group action to be sensitized beforehand to the existence of sexism in textbooks and children's literature and to its harmful consequences for children's development. This circularity of cause and effect shows that it would be futile to attempt to establish a hard and fast order of priority for target populations to be sensitized. The action to be taken must be aimed at the social fabric as a whole, as in the case of the feminist movements, which, having been the first to notice sexism in school textbooks and children's literature, have organized all sorts of action directed both at the school system and at groups outside it. In the cause of greater justice and equality between the sexes, assistance from any quarter should not be spurned. Furthermore, one might well argue that action to prevent sexism in school textbooks and children's literature is easier to carry out and more effective than action to eradicate the harmful consequences of that sexism on the attitudes and conduct of children, parents, educators, and society as a whole. Prevention is always less costly than cure, in both human and financial terms. In this connection, it should be noted that by publishing research work carried out at its request on sexism in the portrayal of women in the media [9], Unesco has already drawn attention to the danger of sexist messages. Bearing this in mind, it is surely inconceivable to guard against sexism in school textbooks and children's books unless, at the same time, its occurrence is prevented in the texts and images of the media.

Conclusion

The studies prepared at Unesco's request on which this work is based have shown that sex stereotypes exist, to a varying degree, in children's literature and school textbooks in all the countries surveyed. The authors of the studies stress the need to launch or to continue sustained action in order to stamp out sexist stereotypes which, through their adverse influence on children of both sexes, create an environment conducive to unequal development in their family, social and working lives. Against this background, the ministers of education in many countries have expressed interest in the preparation of an analytical checklist to identify sex stereotypes and guidelines to assist authors, illustrators and publishers in producing non-sexist works. The checklist would be used to identify and hence to condemn sexist stereotypes while fostering collective awareness of this issue, and the guidelines would promote the production of non-sexist works and develop a spirit of equality and mutual respect between men and women.

This book has sought to comply with that wish by describing certain particularly worthwhile projects that have already been implemented and a range of activities that may help to solve the problem of sexist prejudice.

While it is incumbent on everyone concerned to join in the struggle against sexist prejudice, allowance must be made for the diversity of systems of government. Although the main objective is the same, nevertheless the forms of action taken will differ in free-market economies, where the private sector plays a very important role in the preparation and production of children's literature and school textbooks, and in countries with planned economies, where decisions are made by the appropriate authority and publishing houses are state controlled.

In countries with free-market economies, special attention must be paid to activities that set out to educate, enlighten and persuade different categories of social agent (parents, teachers, authors, illustrators, publishers, etc.). As stressed in the *Born Free* programme in the United States, each individual must realize that he or she can become an agent of change. It must first be understood that all kinds of sexist prejudice may be revealed, perhaps unconsciously, through a person's behaviour. Before convincing others of the need to eliminate sexist prejudice, therefore, one must first rid oneself of any such attitudes or habits. New values and innovative behaviour must then be promoted in the family, at school and in social and occupational circles. Support should be given to the feminist movements, which have emerged in free market economies as a new political force capable of achieving radical change in the social structure. The authorities can contribute effectively to such change by amending existing legislation to eliminate any discrimination based on sex and to promote positive action to enhance equality.

In countries with planned economies, the state can intervene directly when it decides to tackle the problem of sexist prejudice, because it controls the publishing houses and the distribution networks for children's literature and school textbooks. Much progress has certainly been made, but the legacy of the past still persists. This being the case, the Chinese and Ukrainian studies show that the national authorities in those countries attach great importance to preventive action by circulating recommendations to authors, illustrators and publishers.

Best of all would be a combination of planned action by the public authorities with numerous decentralized and private initiatives, either by individuals or by a whole range of associations. This in itself would indicate that society as a whole is aware of the problem of sexism and is trying to find a solution. In Norway, for example, persistent and effective action by feminists since 1970 has been concomitant with the introduction of a system of approval by the Norwegian Government, which authorizes persons designated by the Ministry of Church and Education to refuse to allow sexist school textbooks to be used. These individuals are entitled to ask the authors of the textbooks to remove sexist passages and illustrations prior to their use in schools. The system is not deemed incompatible with the creative freedom of teachers. Politicians and the general public must join forces in the cause of safeguarding human rights, and the defence of the dignity of girls and women is an integral part thereof. There can be no defence of human freedoms as long as such freedoms are viewed solely as the means whereby the dominant perpetuate their oppression of the dominated.

In almost all societies today, men still exercise power and hold sway over women, if not always in the family, then at least in the economy and in politics, religion and culture. It has been shown, also, that while prejudice initially stems from the domination of one human group by another, and serves to justify that domination, prejudice itself subsequently maintains, reproduces and entrenches discriminatory practices and the structures of domination. It may therefore be concluded that when the dominant sex calls for freedom to produce and circulate sexist writings and illustrations, it is striving, whether consciously or unconsciously, to maintain the status quo which establishes its superiority over the other sex.

States seeking to abolish racial prejudice have prohibited its expression in writing and illustration. Why not do the same in the case of sexist prejudice? If the banning of racial prejudice from writing and illustration is deemed to be compatible with authors' freedom of expression in societies seeking to eliminate racism, why should not the banning of sexist prejudice from writing and illustration be compatible with such freedom in societies which believe they must hold the two sexes in equal esteem and abolish the inferior status and subjugation of girls and women? Those members of society who are most keenly aware of the undesirable consequences of sexism should look into this matter more deeply and reinforce statements of principle on the equality of the sexes with action designed to attain their anti-sexist objective. In doing so, they must take account of the great diversity of cultures, institutions and societies, in order to ensure that such measures will prove effective.

Efforts to rid school textbooks and children's books of these stereotypes are of tremendous importance in pedagogical terms, not only for children but also for the adults who write, publish and use them. But society has a duty to devote special attention to children, who are tomorrow's adults. Contacts with schoolteachers are among children's earliest experiences of the adult world. The illustrations and texts in picture books for infants or school textbooks are among their first cultural encounters. Owing to their great receptiveness to messages from the world around them, children will not develop anti-sexist attitudes and forms of behaviour if the messages they receive are imbued with sexist stereotypes. Conversely, the experiments mentioned above show that anti-sexist training of schoolchildren is indeed effective.

Abolishing sexism in school textbooks and children's books is obviously not enough to eliminate it completely from children's minds and behaviour, but it is a first and necessary step that those working in the education system cannot refuse to take, if their aim is to build a society in which the dignity of girls and women and their equality with boys and men are promoted and made an integral part of children's ideas of right and wrong.

Appendix 1

Unesco series of national studies on portrayal of men and women in school textbooks and children's literature: tentative suggestions for research[1]

Introduction

STATEMENT OF THE PROBLEM

It has been observed that most of the messages conveyed to pupils, students and children by school textbooks and children's literature do not take into full consideration the fact that women's life patterns have changed significantly in recent decades. Indeed, although women of different cultural, social and traditional backgrounds have now proved that they can follow roles and careers which have been traditionally reserved for men, this change has not been fully reflected as yet in school textbooks and children's literature.

With regard to men's increasing participation in roles and careers which have been traditionally regarded as reserved for women, changes have been observed also, but neither are these fully reflected in school textbooks and children's literature.

By ignoring the changes that have in fact taken place, by not playing an active and leading role in the promotion and consolidation of such changes, by not being adjusted to the new situations, certain school textbooks and children's literature continue to convey messages which are most of the time false and out-of-date.

The goals of the United Nations Decade for Women are to promote equality between men and women; women's participation in development efforts; and women's contribution to the strengthening of peace.

It has therefore become urgent that sex stereotyping in school education be eliminated and that school education endeavour to promote positive and egalitarian attitudes between the sexes. This idea was reaffirmed by the World Conference of the United Nations Decade for Women (Copenhagen, July 1980) which 'urges governments to take all necessary measures to eliminate stereotypes on the basis of sex from educational material of all levels'.

Changes can only occur when those responsible for the conception, writing, illustrating, editing and interpretation of school textbooks and children's literature are convinced that the perpetuation of stereotyped sex roles and images does have negative effects on society as a whole.[2]

PURPOSE

The present series of studies is a component of Unesco's long-term programme, which was started in 1967, to promote equal education and training opportunities for girls and women. The study teams will examine children's literature and school textbooks in primary and secondary education in their respective countries in order to:

Find out how males and females have been portrayed differently.

Identify any false images of males and females and any stereotyped sex roles.

1. The study team is not obliged to follow the suggestions contained in this paper (Unesco doc. ED–81/WS/72). It may wish to adopt other methods as it deems appropriate.
2. Certain publishers, such as Fernand Nathan in France, and McGraw-Hill in the United States, have issued guidelines asking authors to avoid the presentation of stereotyped sex images and roles.

87

Suggest ways, means, programmes and strategies to eliminate any such false images and stereotyped sex roles, and to promote equality between the sexes.

The report on the studies of this series will be examined with a view to a wide distribution so as to contribute to the advancement of knowledge in this field, and to stimulate action to combat sexism[1] and to promote positive and egalitarian attitudes between the sexes.

Materials concerned

The texts concerned include children's literature for young readers up to the age of 10 or 12 and school textbooks (e.g. readers, history books, civic education textbooks, social science textbooks, etc.) which are currently and widely used in each country involved.

However, in view of the differences in various countries' situations, each national study team is free to decide on the nature (e.g. readers, history, geography, science and mathematics textbooks, etc.) and the number of selected textbooks for analysis at primary and secondary levels. This selection can be based on various considerations, such as:

Scope or representative character (i.e. books and textbooks used throughout the country or in most of the schools).

Textbooks concerning subjects which occupy an important place in the school programme and timetable.

Textbooks influencing noticeably the development of attitudes and behaviour among children and adolescents.

The reason for this selection should be given in the report which each study team will submit to Unesco.

Methodology

STUDY TEAM

It is suggested that a national study team should comprise at least an equal number of women members among research workers and/or specialists in education and psychology, book illustration, authors, book critics, sociology, women's studies, educational and vocational guidance, etc. The study team should draft the study programme and determine the deadline for each phase. The team could be divided into small working groups as appropriate, and would hold group and plenary meetings as necessary.

COLLECTING MATERIALS

In accordance with the criteria adopted, the study team would collect the materials concerned, list and group them by grade and by subject within each grade.

ANALYSIS OF THE MATERIALS[2]

In setting up criteria and a framework for analysing the materials collected, the study team may wish to concentrate attention on a certain number of fundamental points, such as the following:

Content/slurs

These concern sexist words, statements, modifiers, innuendos, etc., in texts or illustrations (e.g. this girl runs and jumps like a boy; he is as weak as a girl).

Stereotypes

These are biasing elements which do not take into due consideration the wide range of men's and women's individual capacities and aspirations and/or express the notion that all or almost all men or women are the same in some ways, when they are not. Stereotypes may be grouped into various categories, such as:

Family/school roles: for example, fathers are breadwinners, mothers are housekeepers; boys like to play football and girls like to play at skipping; most primary-school teachers are women, school principals are men; boys prefer technical subjects, girls prefer social studies; etc.

Personality traits: for example, boys and men are generally presented as 'creators', 'decision-makers', 'doers', while girls and women are generally presented as 'passive', 'dependent', 'watchers', etc.

Social and political roles: for example, women are community workers, social workers; men are community leaders, political leaders, etc.

Occupational roles: for example, female secretaries, male bosses; male doctors, female nurses; etc.[3]

Other stereotypes.

---

1. For the purpose of this study, it is proposed to use the definition given by Marilyn Frye of Michigan State University, United States: 'Sexism if a term which characterizes anything whatever which creates, constitutes, promotes or exploits any irrelevant or impertinent marking of the distinctions between the sexes.'
2. See sex stereotypes review checklist, Table 1, opposite.
3. See Table 2, page 90, which gives a short list of the usual stereotypes.

Appendix 1

Inadequate representation

Girls and women, as they at present appear in children's literature and school textbooks, are misrepresented and/or under-represented. This misrepresentation or under-representation does have a relationship with the development of sex stereotypes.

ELABORATION OF SEX-STEREOTYPE REVIEW CHECKLIST

It would be necessary for the study team to establish one or more review checklists in order to enter findings, remarks and comments concerning all material analysed. Table 1 gives an example of a review checklist.

CONSIDERATION OF THE RESULTS OF THE REVIEWS

Through group and plenary meetings, the study team would examine the results of the review to see whether further investigation is needed in order to obtain fuller data and information.[1]

CONSULTATIONS WITH GOVERNMENT AUTHORITIES, SCHOOL TEXTBOOK AND CHILDREN'S LITERATURE EDITORS, WOMEN'S ORGANIZATIONS, ETC.

On the basis of the study results and conclusions, the study team would discuss with government authorities, editors of children's literature and school textbooks, women's organizations, etc., possible strategies, measures or actions with a view to eliminating sex stereotypes in children's literature and school textbooks, to introduce positive images on women in these materials, and to promote egalitarian attitudes between the sexes. These measures may include:

Informative and promotional action.

Normative action and policy, such as creation of a commission (or asking the relevant existing com-

---

1. The study team may wish to obtain students' and/or teachers' opinions on the subject of the study by means of interviews or questionnaires, etc. See Table 3, page 81.

TABLE 1. Sex stereotypes review checklist

I. *Review*

1. Title
2. Type of material (i.e. primer, reader, etc.)
3. Language and year of publication
4. Level (i.e. for second grade of first level; for readers from 4 to 6 years old, etc.)
5. Reviewed by:
6. Date:

	Content/Slurs		Stereotypes					
	Words/Statements	Illustrations	Family/School roles	Personality traits	Social and political roles	Occupational roles	Other stereotypes (to be defined)	Other stereotypes
Females[1]								
Males[1]								

II. *Specific comments and remarks* (i.e. how females and males are differently presented; if any of these differences are those which have been emphasized, etc.)

III. *Overall comments, including suggestions for appropriate action against sex stereotypes* (i.e. this material was published in . . . . ; a new policy is now being considered to eliminate sex stereotypes, etc.)

1. In each column, under 'Slurs' and 'Stereotypes', enter the number of times slurs against females and males are cited, and the number of times female and male characters are referred to; enter also slight or severe or none, as appropriate.

mission) to consider the sex stereotyped aspects before authorizing the publication of children's literature and school textbooks.

Action through training.

Co-operation with writers, editors, publishers, teachers' associations, women's organizations, etc.

PREPARATION OF THE COMPREHENSIVE REPORT

Five copies of the comprehensive report concerning each national study should have been submitted to Unesco in English or French by the end of September 1982. This report would cover the following topics, among others:

Introduction, including the study objectives.

Composition of the study team, giving name, position and functions of each member.

Programme of the study.

Choice of the materials analysed.

Implementation of the study, including approaches and findings, and gaps and difficulties if any.

Suggestions as to ways, means, programme, etc., to eliminate sexist images in children's literature and school textbooks, at the primary and secondary levels of education, and to promote positive and egalitarian attitudes.

Conclusion.

TABLE 2. Some sex stereotyped occupations which are not universally applicable

Female occupations	Male occupations
Cashiers	Architects
Charwomen	Bakers
Documentalists	Butchers
Factory workers	Deans of faculties
Farm workers	Dentists
Fashion models	Electricians
Librarians	Electronics specialists
Maids	Engineers
Nursery- and primary-school teachers	Explorers
Nurses	Farm managers, supervisors
Radio or television announcers	Farmers
Sales workers	Fishermen
Secretaries	High-school teachers
Semi-skilled workers	Journalists
Social workers	Machinists
Telephone operators	Mechanics
Typists	Medical doctors
Unskilled workers	Office managers, directors
Waitresses	Plumbers
	Policemen and soldiers
	Radio or television commentators
	Sailors
	School principals
	Skilled workers
	Storemen
	Tailors
	Teachers
	Train, bus and truck drivers

TABLE 3. Suggestions for study teams with a view to elaborating questionnaires and/or plans for interviews

1. *Introduction.* Comprehensive explanations should be elaborated in order to inform the respondents of the aims and objectives of the study.

2. *Teachers and teacher educators.* The following topics may be included in the questionnaire or interviews addressed to this group.

2.1. *Personal data*
   (i) Sex
   (ii) Age
   (iii) Functions or responsibilities
   (iv) Duty station

2.2. *Questions*
   (i) Have you observed any changes in children's literature and school textbooks, since 1975, as far as female and male images are concerned?
   (ii) If affirmative, please describe briefly such changes.
   (iii) If no changes have occurred, please answer the following questions:
   Do you think that changes should take place now?
   What changes do you think are urgent?
   What action/measures should be taken to provoke such changes?
   (iv) Have you discussed with pupils or students the sex stereotyped images contained in school textbooks? What are their attitudes concerning this issue?
   (v) Do you consider that such discussions are necessary? Why?

3. *Specialists of curriculum and textbook development, specialists of educational and vocational guidance, specialists in children's literature, publishers.*

3.1. Same as 2.1 above.

3.2. *Questions*
   (i) Have you had any project, since 1975, regarding elimination of sex stereotypes from children's literature and school textbooks, and promotion of equality between the sexes? If affirmative, please elaborate your reply, including results of evaluation, if any.
   (ii) If such a project has not been undertaken as yet, would you think that it is now fully justified?
   (iii) What other initiatives would you consider important in connection with the objective of this series of studies?

4. *Pupils, students and members of youth organizations.*

4.1. Short and simple introduction.

4.2. *Personal data*
   (i) Sex
   (ii) Age
   (iii) Grade
   (iv) Name and address of school

4.3. *Questions*
   (i) What kind of books do you like to read during leisure time? Which school textbooks do you prefer to read? Give reasons for your preferences.
   (ii) Do you agree with the images generally shown in books (novels) and school textbooks with regard to the presentation of females and males? Why?
   (iii) Have you ever discussed this issue of sexism in novels and school textbooks with your friends of both sexes? What are their general reactions? What are boys' reactions? Girls' reactions?
   (iv) In your opinion what should be done to improve the situation?

Appendix 2

Guidelines for equal treatment of the sexes in McGraw-Hill Book Company publications

Introduction

The guidelines that follow are not rigid or mandatory in their details, nor intended to apply to creative literature. They are intended to suggest to our editors and to authors of reference and educational materials and of books and films for children an attitude and some practical means of expressing it.

We believe that educational and reference materials of this kind should reflect a deep conviction that every human being has a dignity and worth that is her or his own, no more dependent on sex than on race or colour, but rather reflecting that individual's own inner being. We would like to see our educational materials in particular convey to all children a sense of opportunity to develop their individual potentials along whatever lines they choose, free of any limiting stereotypes. What is important is not particular forms of expression as such, but this pervasive sense of equality, personal worth, and the unhindered development of potential.

Particular words and ways of using them, however, do often express such a sense of dignity and equality, or, on the other hand, may betray an insensitivity of which the writer may be quite unaware.

For that reason, we have included in the guidelines a number of words, phrases, and constructions that may imply a sexist bias, and we have suggested some ways of avoiding them. These are not intended to be followed mechanically. It is not necessary to use self-consciously awkward or stilted constructions to achieve non-sexist writing. What we are concerned with is not particular words or phrases in themselves, but the substance of what we publish: the basic concepts of equal human opportunity, dignity and freedom and the best ways to reflect those concepts.

ALEXANDER J. BURKE, JR,
President,
McGraw-Hill Book Company

Guidelines for equal treatment of the sexes

The word sexism was coined, by analogy to racism, to denote discrimination based on gender. In its original sense, sexism referred to prejudice against the female sex. In a broader sense, the term now indicates any arbitrary stereotyping of males and females on the basis of their gender.

We are endeavouring through these guidelines to eliminate sexist assumptions from McGraw-Hill publications and to encourage a greater freedom for all individuals to pursue their interests and realize their potentials. Specifically, these guidelines are designed to make staff members and authors aware of the ways in which males and females have been stereotyped in publications; to show the role that language has played in reinforcing inequality; and to indicate positive approaches toward providing fair, accurate, balanced treatment of both sexes in our publications.

One approach is to recruit more women as authors and contributors in all fields. The writings and viewpoints of women should be represented in quotations and references whenever possible. Anthologies should include a larger proportion of selections by and about women in fields where suitable materials are available but where women are currently under-represented.

Women as well as men have been leaders and heroes, explorers and pioneers, and have made notable contributions to science, medicine, law, business, politics, civics, economics, literature, the arts, sports, and other areas of endeavour. Books dealing with subjects like these, as well as general histories, should acknowledge the achievements of women. The fact that women's rights, opportunities, and accomplishments have been limited by the social customs and conditions of their time should be openly discussed whenever relevant to the topic at hand.

We realize that the language of literature cannot be prescribed. The recommendations in these guidelines, thus, are intended primarily for use in teaching materials, reference works, and non-fiction works in general.

THE ROLES OF WOMEN AND MEN

Men and women should be treated primarily as people, and not primarily as members of opposite sexes. Their shared humanity and common attributes should be stressed—not their gender difference. Neither sex should be stereotyped or arbitrarily assigned to a leading or secondary role.

Avoiding job stereotypes

Though many women will continue to choose traditional occupations such as homemaker or secretary, women should not be typecast in these roles, but shown in a wide variety of professions and trades: as doctors and dentists, not always as nurses; as principals and professors, not always as teachers; as lawyers and judges, not always as social workers; as bank presidents, not always as tellers; as members of Congress, not always as members of the League of Women Voters.

Similarly, men should not be shown as constantly subject to the 'masculine mystique' in their interests, attitudes, or careers. They should not be made to feel that their self-worth depends entirely upon their income level or the status level of their jobs. They should not be conditioned to believe that a man ought to earn more than a woman or that he ought to be the sole support of a family.

An attempt should be made to break job stereotypes for both women and men. No job should be considered sex-typed, and it should never be implied that certain jobs are incompatible with a woman's 'femininity' or a man's 'masculinity'. Thus, women as well as men should be shown as accountants, engineers, pilots, plumbers, bridge-builders, computer operators, television repairers, or astronauts, while men as well as women should be shown as nurses, grade-school teachers, secretaries, typists, librarians, file clerks, switchboard operators, or babysitters.

Women with a profession should be shown at all professional levels, including the top levels. Women should be portrayed in positions of authority over men and over other women, and there should be no implication that a man loses face or that a woman faces difficulty if the employer or supervisor is a woman. All work should be treated as honourable and worthy of respect; no job or job choices should be downgraded. Instead, women and men should be offered more options than were available to them when work was stereotyped by sex.

Life-style

Books designed for children at the pre-school, elementary, and secondary levels should show married women who work outside the home and should treat them favourably. Teaching materials should not assume or imply that most women are wives who are also full-time mothers, but should instead emphasize the fact that women have choices about their marital status, just as men do: that some women choose to stay permanently single and some are in no hurry to marry; that some women marry but do not have children; while others marry, have children, and continue to work outside the home. Thus, a text might say that some married people have children and some do not, and that sometimes one or both parents work outside the home. Instructional materials should never imply that all women have a 'mother instinct' or that the emotional life of a family suffers because a woman works. Instead, they might state that when both parents work outside the home there is usually either greater sharing of child-rearing activities or reliance on day-care centres, nursery schools, or other help.

According to the United States Labor Department statistics for 1972, over 42 per cent of all mothers with children under 18 worked outside the home, and about a third of these working mothers had children under 6. Publications ought to reflect this reality.

Both men and women should be shown engaged in home maintenance activities, ranging from cooking and house-cleaning to washing the car and making household repairs. Sometimes the man should be shown preparing the meals, doing the laundry, or changing the baby, while the woman builds bookcases or takes out the trash.

Career options

Girls should be shown as having, and exercising, the same options as boys in their play and career choices. In school materials, girls should be encouraged to show an interest in mathematics, mechanical skills and active sports, for example, while boys should never be made to feel ashamed of an interest in poetry, art or music, or an aptitude for cooking, sewing or child care. Course materials should be addressed to students of both sexes. For example, home economics courses should apply to boys as well as girls, and shop to girls as well as boys. Both males and females should be shown in textbook illustrations depicting career choices.

When as a practical matter it is known that a book will be used primarily by women for the life of the edition (say, the next five years), it is pointless to pretend that the readership is divided equally between males and females. In such cases it may be more beneficial to address the book fully to women and exploit every opportunity to point out to them a broader set of options than they might otherwise have considered and to encourage them to aspire to a more active, assertive, and policy-making role than they might otherwise have thought of.

Women and girls should be portrayed as active participants in the same proportion as men and boys in stories, examples, problems, illustrations, discussion questions, test items, and exercises, regardless of subject matter. Women should not be stereotyped in examples by being spoken of only in connection with cooking, sewing, shopping and similar activities.

PORTRAYALS: HUMAN TERMS

Members of both sexes should be represented as whole human beings with human strengths and weaknesses, not masculine or feminine ones. Women and girls should be shown as having the same abilities, interests, and ambitions as men and boys. Characteristics that have been traditionally praised in males—such as boldness, initiative and assertiveness—should also be praised in females. Characteristics that have been praised in females—such as gentleness, compassion and sensitivity—should also be praised in males.

Like men and boys, women and girls should be portrayed as independent, active, strong, courageous, competent, decisive, persistent, serious-minded, and successful. They should appear as logical thinkers, problem-solvers, and decision-makers. They should be shown as interested in their work, pursuing a variety of career goals, and both deserving of and receiving public recognition for their accomplishments.

Sometimes men should be shown as quiet and passive, or fearful and indecisive, or illogical and immature.

Similarly, women should sometimes be shown as tough, aggressive and insensitive. Stereotypes of the logical, objective male and the emotional, subjective female are to be avoided. In descriptions, the smarter, braver or more successful person should be a woman or girl as often as a man or boy. In illustrations, the taller, heavier, stronger or more active person should not always be male, especially when children are portrayed.

Descriptions of men and women

Women and men should be treated with the same respect, dignity, and seriousness. Neither should be trivialized or stereotyped, either in text or in illustrations. Women should not be described by physical attributes when men are being described by mental attributes or professional position. Instead, both sexes should be dealt with in the same terms. References to a man's or a woman's appearance, charm or intuition should be avoided when irrelevant.

NO	YES
Henry Harris is a shrewd lawyer and his wife Ann is a striking brunette.	The Harrises are an attractive couple. Henry is a handsome blond and Ann is a striking brunette.
	The Harrises are highly respected in their fields. Ann is an accomplished musician and Henry is a shrewd lawyer.
	The Harrises are an interesting couple. Henry is a shrewd lawyer and Ann is very active in community (or church or civic) affairs.

In descriptions of women, a patronizing or girl-watching tone should be avoided, as should sexual innuendoes, jokes and puns. Examples of practices to be avoided: focusing on physical appearance (a buxom blonde); using special female-gender word forms (poetess, aviatrix, usherette); treating women as sex objects or portraying the typical woman as weak, helpless or hysterical; making women figures of fun or objects of scorn and treating their issues as humorous or unimportant.

Examples of stereotypes to be avoided: scatterbrained female, fragile flower, goddess on a pedestal, catty gossip, henpecking shrew, apron-wearing mother, frustrated spinster, ladylike little girl. Jokes at women's expense—such as the woman driver or nagging mother-in-law clichés—are to be avoided.

Appendix 2

NO	YES
the fair sex; the weaker sex	women
the distaff side	the female side or line
the girls or the ladies (when adult females are meant)	the women
girl, as in: I'll have my girl check that.	I'll have my secretary (or my assistant) check that. (Or use the person's name.)
lady used as a modifier, as in lady lawyer	lawyer (A woman may be identified simply through the choice of pronouns, as in: The lawyer made her summation to the jury. Try to avoid gender modifiers altogether. When you must modify, use woman or female, as in: a course on women writers, or the airline's first female pilot.)
the little woman; the better half; the ball and chain	wife
female-gender word forms, such as authoress, poetess, Jewess	author, poet, Jew
female-gender or diminutive word forms, such as suffragette, usherette, aviatrix	suffragist, usher, aviator (or pilot)
libber (a put-down)	feminist; liberationist
sweet young thing	young woman; girl
co-ed (as a noun)	student (N.B. Logically, co-ed should refer to any student at a co-educational college or university. Since it does not, it is a sexist term.)
housewife	homemaker for a person who works at home, or rephrase with a more precise or more inclusive term
career girl or career woman	name the woman's profession: attorney Ellen Smith; Marie Sanchez, a journalist or editor or business executive or doctor or lawyer or agent
cleaning woman, cleaning lady, or maid	housekeeper; house or office cleaner
The sound of the drilling disturbed the housewives in the neighbourhood.	The sound of the drilling disturbed everyone within earshot (or everyone in the neighbourhood).
Housewives are feeling the pinch of higher prices.	Consumers (customers or shoppers) are feeling the pinch of higher prices.

In descriptions of men, especially men in the home, references to general ineptness should be avoided. Men should not be characterized as dependent on women for meals, or clumsy in household maintenance, or as foolish in self-care.

To be avoided: characterizations that stress men's dependence on women for advice on what to wear and what to eat, inability of men to care for themselves in times of illness, and men as objects of fun (the henpecked husband).

Women should be treated as part of the rule, not as the exception. Generic terms, such as doctor and nurse, should be assumed to include both men and women, and modified titles such as 'woman doctor' or 'male nurse', should be avoided. Work should never be stereotyped as 'woman's work' or as 'a man-sized job'. Writers should avoid showing a 'gee-whiz' attitude toward women who perform competently. ('Though a woman, she ran the business as well as any man', or 'Though a woman, she ran the business efficiently'.)

Women participants in the action

Women should be spoken of as participants in the action, not as possessions of the men. Terms such as pioneer, farmer, and settler should not be used as though they applied only to adult males.

NO	YES
Pioneers moved West, taking their wives and children with them.	Pioneer families moved West. Pioneer men and women (or pioneer couples) moved West, taking their children with them.

Women should not be portrayed as needing male permission in order to act or to exercise rights (except, of course, for historical or factual accuracy).

NO	YES
Jim Weiss allows his wife to work part-time.	Judy Weiss works part-time.

Women should be recognized for their own achievements. Intelligent, daring and innovative women, both in history and in fiction, should be provided as role models for girls, and leaders in the fight for women's rights should be honoured and respected, not mocked or ignored.

LANGUAGE CONSIDERATIONS

In references to humanity at large, language should operate to include women and girls. Terms that tend to exclude females should be avoided whenever possible.

The word 'man' has long been used not only to denote a person of male gender, but also generically to denote humanity at large. To many people today, however, the word 'man' has become so closely associated with the first meaning (a male human being) that they consider it no longer broad enough to be applied to any person or to human beings as a whole. In deference to this position, alternative expressions should be used in place of 'man' (or derivative constructions used generically to signify humanity at large) whenever such substitutions can be made without producing an awkward or artificial construction. In cases where man-words must be used, special efforts should be made to ensure that pictures and other devices make explicit that such references include women.

Here are some possible substitutions for man-words:

NO	YES
mankind	humanity, human beings, human race, people
primitive man	primitive people or peoples; primitive human beings; primitive men and women
man's achievements	human achievements
If a man drove 50 miles at 60 mph . . .	If a person (or driver) drove 50 miles at 60 mph . . .
the best man for the job	the best person (or candidate) for the job
man-made	artificial; synthetic; manufactured; constructed; of human origin
manpower	human power; human energy; workers; work force
grow to manhood	grow to adulthood; grow to manhood or womanhood

Pronouns

The English language lacks a generic singular pronoun signifying he or she, and therefore it has been customary and grammatically sanctioned to use masculine pronouns in expressions such as 'one . . . he', 'anyone . . . he', and 'each child opens his book'. Nevertheless, avoid when possible the pronouns he, him, and his in reference to the hypothetical person or humanity in general.

Various alternatives may be considered:
1. Reword to eliminate unnecessary gender pronouns.

NO	YES
The average American drinks his coffee black.	The average American drinks black coffee.

2. Recast into the plural.

	Most Americans drink their coffee black.

3. Replace the masculine pronoun with one, you, he or she, her or his, as appropriate. (Use 'he or she' and its variations sparingly to avoid clumsy prose.)
4. Alternate male and female expressions and examples.

NO	YES
I've often heard supervisors say, 'He's not the right man for the job', or 'He lacks the qualifications for success'.	I've often heard supervisors say, 'She's not the right person for the job', or 'He lacks the qualifications for success'.

5. To avoid severe problems of repetition or inept wording, it may sometimes be best to use the generic 'he' freely, but to add, in the preface and as often as necessary in the text, emphatic statements to the effect that the masculine pronouns are being used for succinctness and are intended to refer to both females and males.

These guidelines can only suggest a few solutions to difficult problems of rewording. The proper solution in any given passage must depend on the context and on the author's intention. For example, it would be wrong to pluralize in contexts stressing a one-to-one relationship, as between teacher and child. In such cases, the expression he or she or either he or she as appropriate will be acceptable.

Occupations

Occupational terms ending in man should be replaced whenever possible by terms that can include members of either sex unless they refer to a particular person who is in fact male. (Each occupational title suggested below is already in wide use in the United States.)

NO	YES
congressman	member of Congress; representative (but Congressman Koch and Congresswoman Holtzman)
businessman	business executive; business manager
fireman	fire fighter
mailman	mail carrier; letter carrier
salesman	sales representative; salesperson; sales clerk

no	yes
insurance man	insurance agent
statesman	leader; public servant
chairman	person presiding at (or chairing) a meeting; presiding officer; the chair; head; leader; co-ordinator; moderator
cameraman	camera operator
foreman	supervisor

Language that assumes all readers are male should be avoided.

no	yes
you and your wife	you and your spouse
when you shave in the morning	when you brush your teeth (or wash) in the morning

PARALLEL TREATMENT

The language used to designate and describe females and males should treat the sexes equally. Parallel language should be used for women and men.

no	yes
the men and the ladies	the men and the women
the ladies and the gentlemen
the girls and the boys
man and wife	husband and wife

Note that lady and gentleman, wife and husband, and mother and father are role words. Ladies should be used for women only when men are being referred to as gentlemen. Similarly, women should be called wives and mothers only when men are referred to as husbands and fathers. Like a male shopper, a woman in a grocery store should be called a customer, not a housewife.

Names

Women should be identified by their own names (e.g. Indira Gandhi). They should not be referred to in terms of their roles as wife, mother, sister or daughter unless it is in these roles that they are significant in context. Nor should they be identified in terms of their marital relationships (Mrs Gandhi) unless this brief form is stylistically more convenient (than, say, Prime Minister Gandhi) or is paired up with similar references to men.

A woman should be referred to by name in the same way that a man is. Both should be called by their full names, by first or last name only, or by title.

no	yes
Bobby Riggs and Billie Jean	Bobby Riggs and Billie Jean King
Billie Jean and Riggs	Billie Jean and Bobby
Mrs King and Riggs	King and Riggs
Ms King (because she prefers Ms) and Mr Riggs
Mrs Meir and Moshe Dayan	Golda Meir and Moshe Dayan or Mrs Meir and Dr Dayan

Unnecessary reference to or emphasis on a woman's marital status should be avoided. Whether married or not, a woman may be referred to by the name by which she chooses to be known, whether her name is her original name or her married name.

Whenever possible, a term should be used that includes both sexes. Unnecessary references to gender should be avoided.

no	yes
college boys and co-eds	students

Titles

In so far as possible, job titles should be non-sexist. Different nomenclature should not be used for the same job depending on whether it is held by a male or by a female.

no	yes
steward or purser or stewardess	flight attendant
policeman and policewoman	police officer
maid and houseboy	house or office cleaner; servant

Different pronouns should not be linked with certain work or occupations on the assumption that the worker is always (or usually) female or male. Instead either pluralize or use 'he or she' and 'she or he'.

no	yes
the consumer or shopper . . . she	consumers or shoppers . . . they
the secretary . . . she	secretaries . . . they
the breadwinner . . . his earnings	the breadwinner . . . his or her earnings or breadwinners . . . their earnings

Males should not always be first in order of mention. Instead, alternate the order, sometimes using: women and men, gentlemen and ladies, she or he, her or his.

Appendix 3

Recommendations to textbook authors and illustrators, drawn up by Fernand Nathan, publishers, June 1980

All too often, the portrayal of men and women in school textbooks no longer has any bearing on real life today as children know it, and does not offer girls opportunities equal to those of boys.

The following observations are intended to encourage you to exercise very great vigilance in this sphere when you produce your manuscript. To allow sexist connotations and situations to persist in works intended for young (and not so young) schoolchildren is to run directly counter to the educational purpose of such books, intended as they are to open a window on the modern world, to inform and to stimulate thought.

It is imperative to fight against the retention of outdated stereotypes, still rife today, especially in the following three fields.

Men's and women's socio-vocational activities (unequal skills)

It is apparent in this connection that traditional examples in grammar, vocabulary exercises, etc., are particularly discriminatory: there is a much more frequent occurrence of the masculine pronoun *il* in general, and the verbs 'invent', 'work', 'make', 'build', 'repair', 'direct', 'organize', etc., take a masculine subject, while the verbs 'chatter', 'wash', 'cook', etc., often have subjects in the feminine gender.

The portrayal of 'life' and 'the family'

The distribution of the roles and tasks of men and women in modern life, relationships between couples and children, husband and wife, mother and father, etc., is also changing, and account must be taken of this. Here, as in socio-vocational activities, the child will be able to see—and one might describe to the child—a real state of affairs that still fits this traditional picture (statistically there are more men than women in decision-making and managerial jobs, more women than men 'in the kitchen' after a day's work, etc.). But this fact does not justify acceptance of the phenomenon as 'normal'; on the contrary, it is important to make children think (to a more or less sophisticated degree) about the origins and causes of this situation, and to help to introduce new attitudes and patterns of thought.

To stick to the facts is also to recognize the existence, alongside the traditional nuclear family, of a growing minority of women who are bringing up their children single-handed. Does this one model family in reading primers really give a feeling of security to the three or four children in the class whose families do not 'conform'?

The physical, psychological and moral portraits of real or fictional characters

Sexism hits girls and women hard in this sphere (they are coquettish, frivolous, spendthrift, less enterprising, dependent on boys/men/husbands), but it hits boys, too, to whom fatigue, insufficient brilliance, lack of virile heroism are forbidden. Individuals should be shown, not necessarily beings of one sex or the other. These recommendations are valid for all school subjects and all levels, but are particularly important for the child's first books (the 6-to-8 age-group), for all books used in teaching (and even for books published as children's literature).

Without attempting to curtail authors' freedom in their creative work, the publisher must nevertheless insist that these comments be taken into account, to ensure that our textbooks no longer reflect outdated images and no longer help to perpetuate largely obsolete stereotypes.

J. SOLETCHNIK,
Educational Director,
Fernand Nathan

References[1]

** 1. ABU NASR, J.; LORFING, I.; MIKATI, J. *Identification and Elimination of Sex Stereotypes in and from School Textbooks: Some Suggestions for Action in the Arab World.* Paris, Unesco, 1983. (Unesco doc. ED-84/WS/31.) (In English.)
2. DUNNIGAN, Lise. *Analyse des stéréotypes masculins et féminins dans les manuels scolaires au Québec.* Quebec, Gouvernement du Québec, 1982.
3. SHESTAKOV, V. Guide on Identification and Elimination of Negative Sex Stereotypes in School Textbooks and Children's Literature and on Promotion of a Positive Image of Women. Paris, Unesco, 1982. (Unpublished document.)
4. MORRIS, Jan. *Conundrum.* New York, New American Library, Inc., 1974.
** 5. BISARIA, Sarojini. *Identification and Elimination of Sex Stereotypes in and from Educational Programmes and Textbooks: Some Suggestions for Action in Asia and the Pacific.* Paris, Unesco, 1983. (Mimeo, in English.)
6. BLUMER, Herbert. United States of America. *International Social Science Journal* (Paris, Unesco), Vol. 10, No. 3, 1958, pp. 403-47.
7. BLUNDEN, Katherine. *Le travail et la vertu; Femmes au foyer: une mystification de la révolution industrielle.* Paris, Payot, 1982. (Bibliothèque historique.)
8. UNITED NATIONS. DIVISION FOR ECONOMIC AND SOCIAL INFORMATION/DPI. Women 1980. *Newsletter*, No. 3, 1980.
9. GALLAGHER, Margaret. *Unequal Opportunities: The Case of Women and the Media.* Paris, Unesco, 1981.
*10. PEOPLE'S REPUBLIC OF CHINA. MINISTRY OF CULTURE. *Study on Portrayal of Men and Women in Chinese School Textbooks and Children's Literature* (by Chen Zijun et al.). Paris, Unesco, 1983. (Unesco doc. ED-83/WS/22.)
*11. UKRAINIAN SOVIET SOCIALIST REPUBLIC. STATE INSTITUTE OF PEDAGOGY (GORKY INSTITUTE); PEDAGOGICAL RESEARCH INSTITUTE. *Study on Portrayal of Men and Women in School Textbooks and Children's Literature in the Ukrainian Soviet Socialist Republic.* Paris, Unesco, 1982. (Unesco doc. ED-82/WS/109.)
*12. NORWAY. NORWEGIAN MINISTRY OF CHURCH AND EDUCATION. *Study on Portrayal of Men and Women in School Textbooks and Children's Literature in Norway* (by Ingeborg Bjerke et al.). Paris, Unesco, 1983. (Unesco doc. ED-83/WS/45.)
13. BÉREAUD, Susan. Les images masculines et féminines dans les albums pour tout-petits. *L'école des parents* (Paris), November 1974, pp. 16-26.
14. CHOMBART DE LAUWE, Marie-Jo. L'enfant et son image. *L'école des parents* (Paris), No. 3, March 1972, pp. 14-26.
*15. WORLD FEDERATION OF TEACHERS' UNIONS (FRENCH SECTION). *A Study of the Portrayal of Women and Men in School Textbooks and Children's Literature in France.* Paris, Unesco, 1983. (Unesco doc. ED-83/WS/118.)
16. MICHEL, Andrée; BÉREAUD, Susan; LORÉE, Marguerite. *Inégalités professionnelles et socialisation différentielle des sexes.* Paris, CNRS/CORDES, 1975. (Mimeo.)
17. STACEY, Judith; BÉREAUD, Susan; DANIELS, Joan (eds.). *And Jill Came Tumbling After: Sexism in American Education.* New York, Dell, 1974.
18. STRAUS, Jacqueline; STRAUS, Murray. Family Roles and Sex Differences in Creativity in Children in Bombay and Minneapolis. *Journal of*

1. National studies carried out at Unesco's request are marked with one asterisk. Regional guides prepared for Unesco are marked with two asterisks.

References

Marriage and the Family (Lake Mills, Iowa), Vol. 30, February 1968.

19. FALCONNET, Georges; LEFAUCHEUR, Nadine. *La fabrication des mâles*. Paris, Le Seuil, 1975.

*20. ZAMBIA. ZAMBIA NATIONAL COMMISSION FOR UNESCO. *Men and Women in School Textbooks. A National Survey on Sex Biases in Zambian Textbooks in Primary and Junior Secondary Schools and their Implications for Education in Zambia* (by L. P. Tempo). Paris, Unesco, 1984. (Unesco doc. ED–84/WS/25.)

*21. PERU. PERUVIAN COMMISSION FOR CO-OPERATION WITH UNESCO. *L'image de la femme et de l'homme dans les livres scolaires péruviens* (by J. Anderson; C. Herencia). Paris, Unesco, 1983. (Unesco doc. ED–83/WS/93.)

22. COMMISSION OF EUROPEAN COMMUNITIES. *Equality of Education and Training for Girls (10–18 years)*. Brussels, CEC, 1978.

23. SEARS, Pauline S.; FELDMAN, David. Teachers' Interactions with Boys and Girls. In: J. Stacey, S. Béreaud and J. Daniels (eds.), *And Jill Came Tumbling After: Sexism in American Education*. New York, Dell, 1974.

24. MOLLO, Suzanne. *L'école dans la société*. Paris, Dunod, 1970.

*25. KUWAIT. NATIONAL COMMITTEE FOR EDUCATION, SCIENCE AND CULTURE. *Report on Men's and Women's Roles in School Textbooks and Children's Literature* (trans. from Arabic by Ibrahim Abd El-Jawad Ahmed). 1983. (Mimeo.)

26. BARUCH, Grace. Sex Roles Attitudes of Fifth Grade Girls. In: J. Stacey, S. Béreaud and J. Daniels (eds.), *And Jill Came Tumbling After: Sexism in American Education*. New York, Dell, 1974.

27. SEARS, Pauline S.; FELDMAN, David. Teachers' Interactions with Boys and Girls. In: J. Stacey, S. Béreaud and J. Daniels (eds.), *And Jill Came Tumbling After: Sexism in American Education*. New York, Dell, 1974.

28. MACCOBY, Eleanor E.; JACKLIN, Carol N. *The Psychology of Sex Differences*. Stanford, Calif., Stanford University Press, 1974.

29. SKJØNSBERG, Karl. *Kjønnsrollemønster i skandinaviske barne- og ungdomsbøker* [Sex Roles in Scandinavian Literature for Young People]. Copenhagen, Gyldendal, 1977. (In Norwegian, English synopsis.)

30. SAFILIOS-ROTHSCHILD, Constantina. Sex Stereotyping in US Primary and Secondary Schools and Interventions to Eliminate Sexism. In: Council of Europe, *Sex Stereotyping in Schools*. Lisse (Netherlands), Swets & Zeitlinger, 1982.

31. WOMEN ON WORDS AND IMAGES (WOWI). *Dick and Jane as Victims, Sex Stereotyping in Children's Readers*. Princeton, N.J., WOWI, 1972.

32. WEITZMAN, L. J., et al. Sex-role Socialization in Picture Books for Preschool Children. *American Journal of Sociology* (Chicago), Vol. 77, No. 6, 1972, pp. 1125–50.

33. ASSOCIATION POUR UNE ÉDUCATION NON SEXISTE. *Dossier 'Pour une éducation non sexiste'*. Association pour une Éducation Non Sexiste, 14 rue Cassette, 75006 Paris. (Regular updates.)

34. DORRER, Rosemarie. Sex Stereotyping in Austrian Schools. In: Council of Europe, *Sex Stereotyping in Schools*. Lisse (Netherlands), Swets & Zeitlinger, 1982.

**35. HANSEN, L. S.; SCHULTZ, C. *Eliminating Sex Stereotyping in Schools: A Regional Guide for Educators in North America and Western Europe*. Paris, Unesco, 1984. (Unesco doc. ED–84/WS/51.)

36. MINISTÈRE DES DROITS DE LA FEMME. La différence est inscrite dans notre culture: c'est là qu'il faut agir. *Citoyennes à part entière* (Paris), No. 16, 1983, p. 13. (Extracts from the address delivered by Yvette Roudy, 27 November 1982, during the Symposium on Human Rights and Education.)

37. GOUVERNEMENT DU QUÉBEC. *L'école sexiste, c'est quoi?* Gouvernement du Québec, Conseil du Statut de la Femme, Spring 1976.

38. KELLY, Alison. Summary Report. In: Council of Europe, *Sex Stereotyping in Schools*. Lisse (Netherlands), Swets & Zeitlinger, 1982.

39. SHAPIRO, June; KRAMER, Silvia; HUNERBERG, Catherine. *Equal Their Chances: Children's Activities for Non-sexist Learning*. Englewood Cliffs, N.J., Prentice-Hall, 1981. (A Spectrum book.)

40. COUNCIL OF EUROPE. *Sex Stereotyping in Schools*. Lisse (Netherlands), Swets & Zeitlinger, 1982.

41. AYALA FLORES, Ana, et al. *Reducción de costos en la producción de libros de texto: estudio de caso, Perú*. Lima, Instituto Nacional de Investigación y Desarrollo de la Educación (INIDE), 1981.

42. MALFATTO, Monique. Faut-il brûler les manuels scolaires? *Antoinette* (Paris, Confédération Générale du Travail), No. 187, September 1980.

43. SKJØNSBERG, Karl. *Kjønnsroller og miljø i barnelitteratur* [Sex Roles, Environment and Social Classes in Children's Literature]. Oslo, Universitetsforlaget, 1972. (In Norwegian, English synopsis.)

References

44. Ministère des Droits de la Femme. Le sexisme dans les manuels scolaires. *Citoyennes à part entière* (Paris), No. 23, September 1983.
45. Gutiérrez Ruiz, Irène. Sex Stereotyping at School in Spain. In: Council of Europe, *Sex Stereotyping in Schools*. Lisse (Netherlands), Swets & Zeitlinger, 1982.
46. Liljeström, Rita, et al. *Roles in Transition: Report of an Investigation Made for the Advisory Council on Equality between Men and Women*. Stockholm, Liber, 1978.
47. Ministère des Droits de la Femme. Les stages-pilotes. *Citoyennes à part entière* (Paris), No. 22, July/August 1983.
48. Kepner, H. S., Jr; Koehn, L. R. Sex-roles in Mathematics: A Study on the Status of Sex Stereotypes in Elementary Mathematics Texts. *The Arithmetic Teacher* (Reston, Va.), Vol. 24, 1977.
49. *L'image de la femme dans les manuels scolaires et livres d'enfants*. Paris, Délégation Régionale à la Condition Féminine, January 1979.

Select bibliography

AGENCE FEMMES INFORMATION (AFI). *L'école aussi préfère les garçons: dossier de presse*, Paris, AFI (21 rue des Jeûneurs, 75002 Paris), 1981.

AMERICAN INSTITUTE FOR RESEARCH (AIR). *Programs to Combat Stereotyping in Career Choice*. Palo Alto, Calif., AIR, 1980.

ASSOCIATION POUR UNE ÉDUCATION NON SEXISTE. *Texte de présentation*. Paris, Association pour une Éducation Non Sexiste (14 rue Cassette, 75006 Paris).

AYALA FLORES, Ana, et al. *Reducción de costos en la producción de libros de textos: Estudio de caso*. Lima, Instituto Nacional de Investigación y Desarrollo de la Educación (INIDE), 1981.

BALBO, Laura. Women's Dual Life and Access to Intellectual Work: Objective Conditions, Sex Stereotyping, New Goals. In: Council of Europe, *Sex Stereotyping in Schools*. Lisse (Netherlands), Swets & Zeitlinger, 1982.

BINGHAM, M.; EDMONDSON, J.; STRYLER, S.; GUTTENTAG, M. *Choices—A Teen Women's Journal for Life/Career Planning*. Santa Barbara, Calif., Advocacy Press, 1983.

BROCK-UTNE, Birgit; HANKAA, Runa. *Kunnskap uten makt: kvinner som lærere og elever* [Knowledge without Power. Women as Teachers and Pupils], 2nd ed. Oslo, Universitetsforlaget, 1981. (In Norwegian.)

BYRNE, Eileen, M. *The Education and Training of Girls in Ireland*. Brussels, Commission of European Communities, 1978. (Report.)

——. *Equality of Education and Training for Girls (10–18 years)*. Brussels, Commission of European Communities, 1978.

CHOMBART DE LAUWE, Marie-Jo. Convergences et divergences des modèles d'enfants dans les manuels scolaires et dans la littérature enfantine. *Psychologie française* (Paris), No. 3, 1965.

COCHINI, Fausta Giani. Research on Sex Stereotyping—Why Focus on Schools? In: Council of Europe, *Sex Stereotyping in Schools*. Lisse (Netherlands), Swets & Zeitlinger, 1982.

COUNCIL OF EUROPE. *Sex Stereotyping in Schools*. Lisse (Netherlands), Swets & Zeitlinger, 1982.

DECROUX-MASSON, Annie. *Papa lit, Maman coud*. Paris, Denoël-Gonthier, 1979. (Femme.)

DORRER, Rosemarie. Sex Stereotyping in Austrian Schools. In: Council of Europe, *Sex Stereotyping in Schools*. Lisse (Netherlands), Swets & Zeitlinger, 1982.

DUBE, Leela. *Studies on Women in Southeast Asia: A Status Report*. Bangkok, Unesco Regional Office for Education in Asia and the Pacific, 1980.

DUPONT, Béatrice. *Fille ou garçon: la même éducation? Étude sur les programmes scolaires dans le secondaire*. Paris, Unesco, 1980.

FALCONNET, G.; LEFAUCHEUR, N. *La fabrication des mâles*. Paris, Le Seuil, 1975.

FOLLET, C.; WATT, M. A.; HANSEN, L. S. *Born Free. Selected Review of the Literature on Career Development and Sex-role Stereotyping at the Post-secondary Higher Education Level*. Newton, Mass., EDC/WEEAP Distribution Center, 1978. (Project Born Free; Technical Report, No. 3.)

FOXLEY, C. H. *Non-sexist Counselling: Helping Women and Men Redefine their Roles*. Dubuque, Iowa, Kendall/Hunt Publishing Co., 1979.

GUTIÉRREZ RUIZ, I. Sex Stereotyping at School in Spain. In: Council of Europe, *Sex Stereotyping in Schools*. Lisse (Netherlands), Swets & Zeitlinger, 1982.

HANNAN, D. Sex Stereotyping in Irish Post-primary Schools. In: Council of Europe, *Sex Stereotyping in Schools*. Lisse (Netherlands), Swets & Zeitlinger, 1982.

HANSEN, L. S. Counselling Issues Related to Changing Roles of Women and Men in Work and Family. *International Journal for the Advancement of Counselling* (The Hague), Vol. 1, Summer 1979, pp. 67–76.

HANSEN, L. S. Gender and Career. In: N. C. Gysbers et al. (eds.), *Designing Careers: Counselling to Enhance Education, Work and Leisure*. San Francisco, Calif., Jossey-Bass, 1984.

——. New Goals and Strategies for Vocational Guidance and Counselling. *International Journal for the Advancement of Counselling* (The Hague), Vol. 4, Summer 1981, pp. 21–3.

HANSEN, L. S.; KEIERLEBER, D. L. A Collaborative Consultation Model for Career Development and Sex-role Stereotyping. *Personnel and Guidance Journal* (Alexandria, Va.), Vol. 56, No. 7, 1978, pp. 395–9. (Special issue.)

HANSEN, L. S.; PELCAK, Doug; PERRAULT, Gerri; DEGE, Dolores. *Born Free. Training Packet to Reduce Sex-role Stereotyping in Career Development: Elementary Level*. Newton, Mass., EDC/WEEAP Distribution Center, 1978.

HENDERSON, Hazel. *The Reawakening of Eve*. (Tape recording of a paper presented at the Global Futures Conference, Toronto, Ontario, October 1980.)

KALLAB, I. *Hya Tatbokh wa Haw Yakra* [She Cooks, He Reads]. Beirut, Beirut University College, Institute for Women's Studies in the Arab World, 1983. (Monograph No. 3, in Arabic.)

KALLAB, I.; ABU NASR, J.; LORFING, I. Sex Roles Images in Lebanese Textbooks. In: I. Cross and J. Downing (eds.), *Sex Roles Attitudes and Cultural Change*. Dordrecht, D. Riedel Publishing, 1982.

KAUFMAN, Jakob, et al. *Attempts to Overcome Sex Stereotyping in Vocational Education*. University Park, Pa., Pennsylvania State University, Institute for Research on Human Resources, 1976. (Mimeo.)

KELLY, Alison. Research on Sex Differences in Schools in the United Kingdom. In: Council of Europe, *Sex Stereotyping in Schools*. Lisse (Netherlands), Swets & Zeitlinger, 1982.

——. Summary Report. In: Council of Europe, *Sex Stereotyping in Schools*. Lisse (Netherlands), Swets & Zeitlinger, 1982.

——. (ed.). *The Missing Half: Girls and Science Education*. Manchester, Manchester University Press, 1981.

KEPNER, H. S., Jr; KOEHN, L. R. Sex Roles in Mathematics: A Study on the Status of Sex Stereotypes in Elementary Mathematics Texts. *The Arithmetic Teacher* (Reston, Va.), Vol. 24, 1977.

KERR, Barbara A. Raising the Career Aspirations of Gifted Girls. *Vocational Guidance Quarterly* (Alexandria, Va.), Vol. 32, No. 1, September 1983, pp. 37–43.

KLEIN, S. S.; THOMAS, V. G. *Sex Equality in Education*. Washington, D.C., U.S. Government Printing Office, 1981. (National Institute of Education sponsored projects and publications.)

LEAL, Yvone. Research into Sex Stereotyping in Schools in Portugal. In: Council of Europe, *Sex Stereotyping in Schools*. Lisse (Netherlands), Swets & Zeitlinger, 1982.

LOCKHEED, M. *Curriculum and Research for Equality: A Training Manual for Promoting Sex Equality in the Classroom*. Princeton, N.J., Educational Testing Service, 1977.

MACCOBY, E. E.; JACKLIN, C. N. *The Psychology of Sex Differences*. Stanford, Calif., Stanford University Press, 1974.

MCGRAW-HILL. *Guidelines for Equal Treatment of the Sexes in McGraw-Hill Book Company Publications*. New York, McGraw-Hill, 1972.

MANSILLA, A.; MARIA, E. *La socialización y los estereotipos sexuales: Estudios de los textos escolares de E.B.R.* Lima, Pontificia Universidad Católica del Perú, 1981. (Mimeo.)

MEER, C. G. *Sex Roles Stereotyping in Occupational Choices: A Career Counselling Manual*. New Brunswick, N.J., Rutgers University, Institute of Management and Labor Relations, 1982.

MICHEL, Andrée. Sex Differentiated Socialization in French Schools. In: Council of Europe, *Sex Stereotyping in Schools*. Lisse (Netherlands), Swets & Zeitlinger, 1982.

MICHEL, Andrée; BÉREAUD, Susan; LORÉE, Marguerite. *Inégalités professionnelles et socialisation différentielle des sexes*. Paris, CNRS/CORDES, 1975. (Mimeo.)

MOLLO, Suzanne. *L'école dans la société*. Paris, Dunod, 1970.

MOTTIER, Z. Sex-role Stereotyping in Textbooks: The Dutch Handrover Project. In: Council of Europe, *Sex Stereotyping in Schools*. Lisse (Netherlands), Swets & Zeitlinger, 1982.

NATIONAL EDUCATIONAL ASSOCIATION (NEA). *Non-sexist Education for Survival*. Washington, D.C., NEA, 1975.

NATIONAL INSTITUTE OF EDUCATION (NIE). *Sex Equality in Education*. Washington, D.C., Department of Health, Education and Welfare, 1980. (National Institute of Education sponsored projects and publications.)

PENN, P. *Evaluation of 1978 Born Free*. Minneapolis, Minn., University of Minnesota, 1978. (Project Born Free, Technical Report, No. 10.)

POGREBIN, L. C. *Growing up Free: Raising your Kids in the 80's*. New York, McGraw-Hill, 1980.

RAPEZA, R. S.; BLOCHER, D. H. The Cinderella Effect: Planning Avoidance in Girls. *Counselling and Values* (Alexandria, Va.), Vol. 21, No. 1, 1976, pp. 12–19.

Romm, T. Interaction of Vocational and Family Factors in the Career Planning of Teenage Girls—A New Developmental Approach. *Interchange* (Toronto), Vol. II, No. 1, 1980/81, pp. 13–24.

Sadken, M. P.; Sadken, D. M. *Sex Equality Handbook for Schools*. New York/London, Longman Inc., 1982.

Safilios-Rothschild, C. Sex Stereotyping in U.S. Primary and Secondary Schools and Interventions to Eliminate Sexism. In: Council of Europe, *Sex Stereotyping in schools*. Lisse (Netherlands), Swets & Zeitlinger, 1982.

Shapiro, J.; Kramer, S.; Hunerberg, C. *Equal their Chances: Children's Activities for Non-sexist Learning*. Englewood Cliffs, N.J., Prentice-Hall, 1981. (A Spectrum book.)

Sheridan, E. M. *Sex Stereotypes and Reading: Research and Strategies*. Newark, Del., International Reading Association, 1982.

Skjønsberg, K. *Kjønnsrollemønster i skandinaviske barne- og ungdomsbøker* [Sex Roles in Scandinavian Literature for Young People]. Copenhagen, Gyldendal, 1977. (In Norwegian, English synopsis.)

——. *Kjønnsroller og miljø i barnelitteratur* [Sex Roles, Environment and Social Class in Children's Literature]. Oslo, Universitetsforlaget, 1972. (In Norwegian, English synopsis.)

——. *Velg selv. Ungdom, utdanning og kjønns-roller* [Freedom to Choose: Youth, Education and Sex Roles]. Oslo, Likestillingsrådet, 1981.

Spender, D. The Role of Teachers: What Choices do they Have? In: Council of Europe, *Sex Stereotyping in Schools*. Lisse (Netherlands), Swets & Zeitlinger, 1982.

Spender, D.; Payne, I. *Learning to Lose: Sexism and Education*. London, The Women's Press, 1980.

Stacey, J.; Béreaud, S.; Daniels, J. (eds.). *And Jill Came Tumbling After: Sexism in American Education*. New York, Dell, 1974.

Tornes, K. Sex Stereotyping and Schooling: A General Overview. In: Council of Europe, *Sex Stereotyping in Schools*. Lisse (Netherlands), Swets & Zeitlinger, 1982.

Tornieforth, G. Sex Stereotyping in German School Education. In: Council of Europe, *Sex Stereotyping in Schools*. Lisse (Netherlands), Swets & Zeitlinger, 1982.

United Nations. *Women and the Media*. New York, 1982.

Verheyden-Hilliard, M. E. *A Handbook for Workshops on Sex Equality in Education*. Washington, D.C., American Personnel and Guidance Association, 1976.

Veya, E. Research into Sex Stereotyping in School in Switzerland. In: Council of Europe, *Sex Stereotyping in Schools*. Lisse (Netherlands), Swets & Zeitlinger, 1982.

Warsett, S. *Evaluation Report on Born Free Videotapes, Training Packet and Selected Workshops*. Minneapolis, Minn., University of Minnesota, 1978. (Project Born Free, Technical Report, No. 9).

Weitzman, L.; Eifler, D.; Hokada, E.; Ross, C. Sex-role Socialization in Picture Books for Pre-school Children. *The American Journal of Sociology*, Vol. 77, No. 6, May 1972.

Wernersson, I. Sex Differentiation and Teacher/Pupil Interaction in Swedish Compulsory School. In: Council of Europe, *Sex Stereotyping in Schools*. Lisse (Netherlands), Swets & Zeitlinger, 1982.

Wolpe, A. M. *Woman's Occupational Choice: The Impact of Sexual Divisions in Society*. Stockholm Institute of Education, Department of Educational Research, 1980. (Reports on Education and Psychology, No. 3.)

Women on Words and Images (WOWI). *Dick and Jane as Victims: Sex Stereotyping in Children's Readers*. Princeton, N.J., WOWI, 1972.

[A.ED.85/D-151/A]